Freewriting with **Purpose**

Simple classroom techniques to help students make connections,
think critically, and construct meaning

Karen Filewych

Pembroke Publishers Limited

To Kevin and Ken:
For your unconditional love and support

© **2019 Pembroke Publishers**
538 Hood Road
Markham, Ontario, Canada L3R 3K9
www.pembrokepublishers.com

Distributed in the U.S. by Stenhouse Publishers
www.stenhouse.com

Funded by the Government of Canada
Financé par le gouvernement du Canada | Canada

Library and Archives Canada Cataloguing in Publication

Filewych, Karen, author
    Freewriting with purpose : simple classroom techniques to help students make connections, think critically, and construct meaning / Karen Filewych.

Includes bibliographical references and index.
Issued in print and electronic formats.
ISBN 978-1-55138-339-2 (softcover).--ISBN 978-1-55138-939-4 (PDF)

    1. English language--Writing--Study and teaching (Elementary). 2. English language--Composition and exercises--Study and teaching (Elementary). 3. Creative writing (Elementary education). I. Title.

LB1576.F452 2019   372.62'3   C2018-905906-0
                                            C2018-905907-9

Editor: Kate Revington
Cover Design: John Zehethofer
Typesetting: Jay Tee Graphics. Ltd.

Printed and bound in Canada
9 8 7 6 5 4 3 2 1

Contents

Acknowledgments

I am fortunate to love what I do each day, but I don't do it alone. I thank the educators I work with: Your passion for learning and teaching are exhilarating. I thank the students I teach: Your genuine joy and enthusiasm are contagious.

Thanks also go

- to Greg and Susana, for sharing your experiences and perspective
- to Laurie and Dan, for your support of my work in your schools and for steering me down a new path
- to my faithful readers, Katrina, Christina, Cheryl, Erin, Tannis, and especially Mom, for your time and insight
- to the Pembroke team — in particular, Mary Macchiusi, my publisher, and Kate Revington, my editor — for pushing me to new heights

Most of all, I give thanks to my family, especially Dan, for understanding that deadlines need to be met and for supporting my dream, always.

Introduction: Freewriting into Understanding

"Literacy is not a luxury; it is a right and a responsibility."
— Bill Clinton

What are your goals as a classroom teacher? Regardless of the age of your students or the subjects you teach, I would expect to hear answers like these:

- to motivate and engage students
- to develop students' thinking skills
- to teach students *how* to learn
- to help students reach their potential
- to empower students as readers and writers
- to help develop literate, contributing, empathetic members of society
- to inspire students to find meaning and purpose in life

In any event, these are my goals as a classroom teacher. Perhaps the order would change on a given day, but these are my ultimate goals. Furthermore, each year, as I gain experience, learn from those around me, and develop new strategies, my goals become better defined and I come closer to reaching them.

Connecting Freewriting to Classroom Goals

Many strategies, techniques, and approaches have made my teaching practice stronger. The most significant, though, was the introduction of freewriting into my classroom. Unexpectedly, this process helped me reach all the goals I have for the students in my classroom. I admit that, as a writer, I may be a bit biased about its impact. Yet I know that others agree on its potential to enhance student learning. As ReLeah Cossett Lent (2016) has said, "If there is a learning elixir, it may well be writing" (63).

How did freewriting come about in my classroom? I first encountered it as a writer, not as a teacher. This process helped me put words on paper more easily and more consistently. As a teacher, I watched many of my students struggling to write, and I wondered if this technique could benefit them, as well. *Writing with Power* by Peter Elbow and *Writing Down the Bones* by Natalie Goldberg both speak to the idea of freewriting. Elbow names it thus; Goldberg speaks to the process without using the term. Before exploring what is involved in the process — Chapter 1 will do that in detail — let's explore why it is effective for our students. Elbow (1998) talks about two types of writers:

… ordinary writers fall into two camps. Either creativity has won out and produced writers who are rich but undisciplined, who can turn out lots of stuff with good bits in it, but who are poor at evaluating, pruning and shaping. Or else critical thinking has won out and produced writers who are careful but cramped. They have great difficulty writing because they see faults in everything as they are trying to put it down on paper. (9)

He goes on to say:

But you don't have to give in to this dilemma of creativity versus critical thinking and submit to the dominance of one muscle and lose the benefits of the other. If you separate the writing process into two stages, you can exploit these opposing muscles one at a time: first be loose and accepting as you do fast early writing; then be critically toughminded as you revise what you have produced. What you'll discover is that these two skills used alternately don't undermine each other at all, they enhance each other. (9)

When I made the connection to my classroom, this two-stage process made perfect sense: first, we teach students how to get their words on paper, and *then*, we teach them how to enhance their work through revision. Separately. "The aim is to burn through to first thoughts," as Goldberg (2005, 8) puts it, and then, later, spend time talking about our writing and how to *improve* those first thoughts.

The result in my classroom was astonishing. My students and I were able to break through many of the barriers they faced — fear, reluctance, and insecurities about writing — using this simple technique. They gained confidence in their abilities and became excited by writing and its possibilities. Perhaps most telling, my students — even those previously most reluctant — began *asking* to freewrite.

I was teaching Grade 6 when I first introduced freewriting into my classroom. It evolved somewhat each year I used it, but I quickly realized that this process was effective at any grade level I was teaching. It truly didn't matter if the students were 7, 11, or 17 years old or if they were adult learners. Freewriting worked.

Freewriting across Subject Areas

At first, my students and I were freewriting only within my language arts program. Eventually it dawned on me I could use this process not only to improve my students' writing and attitudes towards writing, but to help them learn and construct meaning in all curriculum areas. I then identified the two distinct purposes of writing in my classroom: (1) *learning to write* and (2) *constructing meaning*.

Once I recognized this distinction, my students and I began freewriting in social studies, in mathematics, in science, in art class, and in health. Although our education systems tend to divide the disciplines and expect subjects to be taught isolated from each other, these subject areas are interconnected. As Dennis Littky (2004) suggests, "What is science without math? What is history without language? What are languages without their history?" (29). In fact, Littky believes that we should *overhaul the entire structure of schools* (29). I, too, believe that the subject areas are profoundly interconnected. In my mind, elementary teachers have an advantage in that they spend most of the day with the same group of students and teach most disciplines of study. There is, therefore, more flexibility in planning and an ongoing opportunity to connect the various disciplines. In

To better address the purpose of this book, I have separated chapters 6 through 11 by discipline to reflect the way that most of our classrooms and schools are structured.

junior high and high school, teachers are typically specialists in one subject area and students have various teachers throughout their day, making the integration of subject areas more challenging. But regardless of the grade level or subject you teach, I believe that freewriting can be successfully integrated into your classroom.

Developing Disciplinary Literacy

Teachers of content-area curriculum often worry that they are not prepared to teach writing to their students. Yet literacy grounds every discipline of study in provincial or state curriculums: in fact, the term *disciplinary literacy* is becoming more and more common. As Lent (2016) says in her book about the topic: "The good news is that you don't need to be a teacher of writing. You only need to show your students how scientists, mathematicians, historians, poets, musicians, or sports writers — whoever writes in your discipline — communicate through writing" (78). As she describes it here, this is *learning to write* as connected to a specific discipline. In addition, though, writing can be used as a tool to deepen our students' understanding of the content: *constructing meaning*.

Understanding Subject Content

Often, after teaching a lesson, watching a video, or reading a book, we engage our students in discussion to further their understanding. But really, how many students participate in the discussion? Three? Four? Five? And wouldn't you say it's typically the same students who participate? In reality, we want *all* students to engage in the content: something discussion alone does not usually facilitate. By *writing* about the lesson, the video, or the book, all students tend to engage with and therefore understand the content more profoundly. In fact, through writing they often connect to the content rather than simply memorizing the information. Whereas memorization tends to result in forgetting the content as soon as the class is over or the test, written, understanding tends to lead to deeper learning and, therefore, greater retention — an internalization of the material, if you will. By freewriting across the curriculum, we use writing as a form of thinking and a way of knowing. Rather than it being an add-on to the content, it becomes an indispensable process on the learning journey.

A Way to Find Joy in Writing

Not only do I want students to write more and write well, I want them to find joy in writing. When our students are in Grade 1, most of them are excited about writing and the possibilities before them — this is a newfound form of communication. But as our students get older, many of them do not take pleasure in the process. And for the ones that do ... it's just not "cool" to admit it. Perhaps their displeasure with writing comes from the way we teach it.

My desire to inspire students and build confidence in teachers motivates me to sit at my computer and write about my trials and successes with this process. I unequivocally share the conviction of Kelly Gallagher and Penny Kittle (2018, xv): "We believe that the teaching of literacy can be life changing. Literally."

A former colleague, currently teaching Grade 2, admittedly struggles to teach writing. She does not enjoy writing herself and does not feel adept teaching it to her students. The good news? This teacher has told me that through use of freewriting, she now feels both confident and competent teaching writing to her class. When I asked her why this technique works for her, she said she finds the method accessible and not intimidating: the writing time is short, and the process, easy to implement. She now realizes that she doesn't have to be the best *writer* to teach writing. She can motivate her students to write, and then, one by one, teach the skills needed to improve their writing. I have received similar responses from many other educators since.

Freewriting as Part of School Culture

My experience as an administrator has confirmed for me that when we set goals for our school, most often, we include a literacy goal. Reading and writing remain critical for our students' success in school and, even more important, in life. Serving as an administrator has also taught me that when we share a vision and work towards these goals together, we are more successful in reaching them.

One reason freewriting is so effective is precisely because it can be used by teachers in all areas of the curriculum; however, its value is not always readily apparent. In our school district, for example, we have elementary music specialists. As I was preparing for a teacher workshop, the principal asked if she should invite the music teacher to our session. Music teachers are often excluded from core professional development because it is not applicable to their discipline. And yet, even in music class, the process of freewriting can enhance the curriculum and our students' learning. When we invite our teachers to see how freewriting can be used as a way to construct meaning, it becomes applicable to students of all age levels and to curriculum in all areas.

Freewriting can be used independently within our classrooms, but the best results come when all teachers within a school begin to use this process — when it becomes intrinsic in the culture.

The Game Changer

To motivate and engage students. To develop students' thinking skills. To teach students how *to learn. To help students reach their potential. To empower our students as readers and writers. To help develop literate, contributing, empathetic members of society. To inspire students to find meaning and purpose in life.*

To my amazement, freewriting helped me achieve all these goals of mine on a deeper level — my students' learning intensified. Now I cannot imagine my classroom without freewriting regardless of the grade level, the subject, the time of day, or the time of year. My simple decision to explore the use of this technique with my 10- and 11-year-old students transformed my teaching. Freewriting is not a difficult process to implement and yet it makes a significant difference in teacher attitudes, student confidence, and, ultimately, in our students' writing abilities. It is not the be-all and end-all of writing in our classrooms, but it is an effective technique to enhance the learning process.

Freewriting was a game changer in my classroom, and I expect that it will be in yours, as well.

1

First Things First

"Fill your paper with the breathings of your heart."
— William Wordsworth

I have heard the term *freewriting* used in different ways to mean different things. For many, freewriting implies that our students are free to write whatever they want. Freewriting, however, is much more than that. In this chapter I explore what the process of freewriting entails, its potential in the classroom, and the most common questions I receive about it.

What is freewriting?

Perhaps the most important component of freewriting is that we write continuously: we begin with a prompt and keep our pen or pencil moving throughout the duration of the freewrite. We do not stop to question or censor ourselves; we do not write what we think someone else wants to hear; we write what comes to mind generated by the prompt. We do not concern ourselves with spelling, punctuation, capitalization, or grammar — all of that will come in time. As Peter Elbow (1998) describes, we separate the creative and critical processes: we do not let the critical thoughts creep into our freewriting time.

Prompt-Based Writing

I appreciate Linda Rief's work on quickwrites. Although freewriting and quickwrites are similar in some ways, there are also important differences. In her book *The Quickwrite Handbook*, Rief (2018) defines a quickwrite as this: "a first draft response to a short piece of writing, usually no more than one page of poetry or prose, a drawing, an excerpt from a novel or a short picture book" (3). Her quickwrites always use a mentor text as a starting point for student writers. As you will see, freewriting does not.

How do we write continuously? How do we teach our students to do this? The key is the prompt. After much experimentation, I have realized that a two-word prompt is most effective at the beginning: "I wish …," "Today I …," or "I remember …" If we or our students get *stuck*, we simply write the prompt again and put down the first thing that comes to mind. The rewriting of the prompt is vital to ensure that our pens or pencils keep moving. Although Elbow speaks about an open-ended process, one in which we write whatever comes to mind, I find the use of a prompt essential to keep my students' pens and pencils moving. Eventually, students may be comfortable with a visual prompt such as a picture or a video, but even then, I provide a prompt of a few words. This practice ensures success for all. Instead of sitting with "nothing to write," students rewrite the prompt and persist. Lo and behold, it works! Students can write continuously.

How do we begin?

Before I introduce the idea of freewriting — no matter the students' age — I engage in a discussion about how students *feel* about writing. I begin by asking, "Who likes to read?" Typically, many hands go up. Then I ask, "Who likes to write?" Often, especially with older students, some of those hands go down, or the students give me a so-so gesture. And that's when we explore the reasons *why*. I ask, "So, what don't you like about writing?" Common answers tend to surface:

"I'm not a good writer."

"I don't know *what* to write."

"I don't know how to spell."

"I'm afraid of making mistakes."

"I have nothing to say."

"I don't want anyone to read my writing."

Although the wording may be different, these answers — and the sentiments behind them — emerge regardless of the age of the students. Most often, the answers reflect a lack of confidence in their abilities. And while this discussion saddens me somewhat because I realize the current reality of classroom writing, I am always eager to introduce freewriting to students, knowing the impact it will have on both their abilities and their attitudes.

After we discuss our feelings towards writing, I explain we are going to try a method of writing that will help them get words on paper without worrying about mistakes, spelling, or ideas. I even explain how we will try to separate our creative and critical thinking brains for this process.

I use the prompt "I remember …" for their first freewriting experience as it tends to be most effective in engaging them in the process. After all, we all remember something!

How long do we freewrite?

Regardless of the age of my students, the first freewriting experiences tend to be between five and seven minutes long. This time frame may seem surprisingly short, but I want to ensure that the first few experiences are positive. For everyone. Pushing the time frame longer can lead to frustration or feelings of failure if students can't keep their pencils or pens moving. I set a stopwatch on my phone (counting up, not down) to keep beside me. Because I am writing with my students, I keep an eye on both the stopwatch and the students. If I see a few students slowing down, I may quietly remind the group, "Keep your pencils moving." Or, I'll tell them, "Rewrite the prompt if you get stuck." When we get past six minutes, I observe the energy in the room. If most students are still writing furiously (or even moderately), I will persist. If more than a couple are slowing down, I will give a warning, "Okay, writers. Let's push through for one more minute."

Read the Room

Over time, as students become accustomed to the process and as I get to know them, I will increase the writing time, if only by a minute or two each time. But we never get to a point where students find the amount of time painful. "You have to write long enough to get tired and get past what's on top of your mind. But not so long that you start pausing in the midst of your writing," advises Elbow (1998,

I also share this with students: *Even though I like to write, I still find it difficult and challenging; it is an ongoing learning process.*

51). You may find that some prompts better engage a particular group on a given day than others. If the goal is to help students experience success with writing, we must read the room. We can push longer if they are engaged, but we should stop sooner if they seem to be slowing.

Although this writing time is short, think about a typical writing assignment you give to your students. Have they even started putting pen to paper within six or seven minutes? Some, yes, but certainly not all of them. That initial time after an assignment is given is often pencil-sharpening time, bathroom time, drink-of-water time: avoidance! With freewriting, however, students will have a surprising amount of writing on their pages within six or seven minutes.

Why do I write with my students and urge you to do so, too?

As you may have noticed, I write with my students. Part of what makes this process successful is that we, as teachers, engage in the writing process. This thought gives many teachers immediate anxiety. Stay with me. If we expect our students to make themselves vulnerable through writing, then we should be willing to write with them. Just like our students, many teachers, too, feel that they are not strong writers. But sincerely I tell you, if you are willing to take the risk, you will notice several advantages of engaging in this process with your students.

The first benefit of writing with students is that it sets the tone for the freewrite. Some students want our attention when they want it. But when students see us writing, they realize this isn't the time for questions or washroom breaks: this is the time to write. *Everyone* is writing. Immediately they learn to honor the time. For those of us who teach the younger students, we know the most common question during writing time is "How do you spell …?" Before we begin, I say to my students: "Can you ask me how to spell something while we are writing? No, because I will be busy writing, too. Do your best and keep going." It works!

The second benefit of writing with students is that they will realize that their writing and ours does not have to be perfect or brilliant as we put pen to paper. Recognizing that writing begins raw and rough is important for students to understand. Writing is thinking. Writing is a craft that requires work for all of us. I certainly wouldn't want the first draft of this manuscript published: it is rough, sometimes stream-of-consciousness, random thoughts that still require much revision and time. When I show or read my own freewriting, students understand that what I am sharing is first thoughts: first thoughts that can be improved upon later, if I choose. That is a freeing concept.

The third benefit of writing with students is that we become learners together. I can say to my students with sincerity, "When I was writing today …" or "When I wrote this piece, I noticed …" When we write, too, we truly become engaged in the learning process along with our students. Just as students appreciate it when we play soccer alongside them in physical education class, they also appreciate it when we read and write, take risks, and learn alongside them.

Understanding from Within

Still not convinced? Donald Graves and Penny Kittle (2005) quote Donald Murray in their book *Inside Writing*:

Teachers should write, first of all, because it is fun. It is a satisfying activity that extends both the brain and the soul. It stimulates the intellect, deepens the experience of living, and is good therapy. Teachers should write so they understand the process of writing from within. They should know the territory intellectually and emotionally: how you have to think to write, how you feel when writing. Teachers of writing do not have to be great writers, but they should have frequent and recent experience in writing. If you experience the despair, the joy, the failure, the success, the work, the fun, the drudgery, the surprise of writing you will be able to understand the composing experiences of your students and therefore help them understand how they are learning to write. (p. 1, DVD viewing guide)

Take the plunge: write with your students!

What about sharing our work?

As I said, I give my students a warning as we come to the end of our writing time: "Okay, writers. Let's push through for one more minute." At the end of this minute, I say: "Grade 4 writers, please finish the sentence you are on and then quietly read your work to yourself." I build this routine into every freewrite experience. After we have all read our work quietly to ourselves, I give students the options of sharing *all*, *some*, or *none* of the writing out loud. I, as the teacher, have the same options. This choice to share or not is critical in the success of freewriting in your classroom: having this control liberates students during the writing process. They are not worried about censoring themselves or someone reading their work; therefore, their writing is truly more spontaneous and less inhibited. I am careful to keep the promise of letting students share *all*, *some*, or *none* of their work, respecting their choices on each particular day.

How to Model Thinking about Sharing

To help establish an appropriate environment and tone for our sharing time, I find it effective to model my own thought process for sharing my work. Depending on what I have written, I might say:

- "Today using our prompt, I wrote about three different things: the first day of school, my dog, and my brother. Today I'm going to read you the part about my brother."
- "Today I wrote about my dad's illness. It's quite personal and I've decided not to share my writing this morning."
- "Today I wrote about the day my dad died. I'm going to share it with you and I know everyone will be respectful."

In the first example, I might also explain that if I was going to work on this piece as something to be published, I wouldn't have to include the whole freewrite; I would take this part about my brother, revise it, and likely add to it. Students will see that my thoughts moved from idea to idea during my freewrite and understand that that's *okay*. This conversation is nonthreatening and effective because it is about my writing.

When I share writing that is somewhat personal or emotional, students are always incredibly sensitive and respectful. This sharing sets the tone for the inevitability of a student sharing an experience such as this. I want them to know it is acceptable not to share if they do not feel comfortable; I also want them to know that they are in a safe environment if they do decide to share something painful or personal.

How to Go About Sharing

Chapter 2 discusses the process of sharing in more detail.

Although I model my thought process for deciding whether I want to share a certain piece of writing, I encourage my students not to say anything before reading their work out loud to the class. Some students tend to justify or apologize for the quality of their work or the fact that they may not have "finished." I remind them there is no need for an apology: we all realize that they have spent only six or seven minutes writing this piece. Some students want to talk about what they wrote *instead* of reading their writing out loud. Right from the beginning, I set the expectation that we are not talking *about* our writing but *reading* it out loud.

Can students use computers or tablets during a freewrite?

I have experimented with freewriting on digital devices, sometimes having students use them during their first freewriting experience and sometimes after students are familiar with the process. As much as I love technology, in this situation, the device gets in the way of the process. Students tend to write less and there is more of a temptation to stop and correct what they are writing. That separation between the creative and critical processes of the brain becomes more difficult when using technology: the computer literally alerts us to our mistakes.

A Preference for Paper

Initially, therefore, I prefer that during a freewrite, all students write on paper. There is something more physical and more personal about the pen-to-paper experience. Typically, too, pen to paper is faster for many of our students who have not yet mastered the skill of typing. I know that the creative, authentic, emotional part of my brain works better on paper. And most students, even in this digital age, have shared this preference as well.

If and when your students decide to revise and edit a freewrite, they can then use the computer or tablet to work on their pieces further. Technology has its place. After all, I cannot imagine writing, revising, and editing this manuscript without my computer.

If, in time, you notice a student who, you think, would benefit from freewriting on a device, invite that student to try it. If the experience is positive, allow this individual to continue using the device. But keep in mind, in all the years I have taught freewriting, only a few students have chosen a device, and those who did had fine motor challenges preventing their hands from keeping up with their brain.

For a select few over the years, I have also found success using dictation software.

Do we assess freewriting?

As teachers, we sometimes avoid giving writing assignments, knowing it means another mountain of papers to take home and assess over the weekend. We also tire of reading stacks of student writing all on the same topic: stories, essays, or papers that our students think we want to hear. I know. I used to be one of those teachers.

One unexpected benefit of the process of freewriting is that the writing I am now assessing is much more interesting to read. Student personalities and their writing voices become more evident through this process. Instead of reading 25 pieces on the same thing, I am reading 25 pieces that are unique and enjoyable to read. And I certainly don't assess everything my students write, which they do almost daily. I had to learn to give myself permission to drop that guilty feeling of not assessing (or reading) everything they write.

Assessment in Moderation

If we were to assess every freewrite our students wrote, we would take away the freedom, intensity, and even the necessary randomness this process allows. Students would then again be worried about what they write as they are writing it. We would defeat the purpose of the entire process. If we *are* going to assess students' freewriting, we give them choice about which piece to submit and provide the opportunity for them to revise and edit their work. We never assess freewriting in its initial raw form.

What about conventions?

My students are always surprised (and delighted) when I tell them that I don't want them to worry about perfect spelling, punctuation, capitalization, or grammar during freewriting. That's not to say we avoid it or deliberately exclude it; we simply do not worry about it. If I don't know how to spell something, I try my best and move on.

I always ask my students, "Do you think that I think conventions are important?" They always know the answer: "Yes!" Conventions *are* important but not yet. Students get their ideas down on paper first (the creative process) and if they decide to publish their writing, they have time to edit their work for conventions later (the critical thinking process). I remind them that we are going to turn our critical thinking brains off during the freewrite and then back on afterwards.

My students quickly learn that I have high expectations for conventions when they submit their work to me; however, they always have time to edit their writing before they hand it in.

Should I buy special journals or notebooks for freewriting?

No. The first year my students and I were freewriting, we wrote on loose-leaf paper. We created a section in our binder titled *Freewriting* and added our page to the section each time we wrote. Despite this system working well, the next year I bought special notebooks for my students' freewriting. It backfired. For several reasons, I think.

First, these *nice-looking journals* made the students reluctant to write what came to mind. The journals made them feel as if their writing should be finished or complete: contrary to how I wanted them to approach this type of writing. The mindset for using the journals was different.

Second, and connected to this, I noticed that the journals made it more difficult to make revisions on the writing we chose to revise. When I used loose-leaf paper, students would take the page out of their binders, bring it to their writing groups to share, and make revisions directly on the paper. Even though we double-spaced journal pages in the same way as we did with loose-leaf paper, the space for revisions felt tight and awkward, and the students didn't want to mark up their pages. It wasn't long before I regretted buying the journals.

Loose-Leaf Paper Is Best

Partway through that year, my students and I returned to loose-leaf paper and used the journals for another purpose. Since that time, I have used loose-leaf paper organized in a section of their binders. I give each student a double-sided tracking sheet to place at the front of the *Freewriting* section in the binder (see the line master on page 21). Each time we finish a freewrite, we date our writing and then fill out the tracking sheet together. This routine prevents the loose-leaf pages from getting lost in the abyss of our students' desks or bins! When freewriting across the curriculum, we either keep all freewriting in one section or create a section in each subject. Either approach will work.

> **What about our especially young students?** In Grade 1, my preference is to use small binders with loose-leaf paper and take the time to train the students to organize their work. This routine requires both our insistence and our patience as teachers. The students can do it; in fact, in time they become surprisingly proficient with the binders as long as we set the expectation. If you feel unready to tackle binders in Grade 1, scribblers would be my second choice.

How do I approach an especially reluctant writer?

Freewriting is successful quite immediately for most students. In fact, one reason I like this process as much as I do is that it engages most of our reluctant writers. Over the years, however, I have encountered a few individuals who, for various reasons, are somewhat harder to reach. Although I may scribe for a student in other circumstances, I tend not to during freewriting. I have three suggestions for especially reluctant writers:

1. *Sit next to the reluctant writer during writing time.* As you both write, you can quietly provide encouragement to that individual as needed: "Just keep your pencil moving ...," "Write whatever comes to mind ...," and "I know you can do it."
2. *Talk openly (and privately) with a student who is not fully participating.* Often, this dialogue is enough to motivate that individual or discover the reason for not writing. Although our students will not likely voice this, fear or low confidence is often what is preventing them from fully engaging.
3. *Try a different kind of prompt.* If you have been using two-word prompts beginning with the word *I* such as "I remember ..." or "I need ...," change it up and try another format such as "My mom ..." or "I wish my parents knew ..." or even "If I were the principal ..." Perhaps students will connect better to a prompt like this.

Persist and stay positive: praise even small gains. The good news? The students who fall in this category are few. The process is immediately effective for most.

What are the benefits of freewriting?

Although the benefits of freewriting are many, I have focused on six main ones in the classroom: (1) breaking down barriers, (2) learning to write, (3) constructing meaning, (4) developing the habit of reading our work, (5) providing differentiation, and (6) expressing what we think and feel.

1. Breaking Down Barriers

As Elbow (1998) explains, "Most people experience an awkward and sometimes paralyzing translating process in writing: 'Let's see, how shall I say this.' Freewriting helps you learn to just say it" (15). This is the benefit I noticed immediately in my classroom: freewriting breaks down the barriers, even for the most reluctant or struggling students. It addresses the reasons some students don't like writing and makes the process of writing less intimidating. Students find both confidence and voice. Why? The element of choice — to share or not to share — liberates our students. The pressure is off. They realize there is no need to be perfect, no need for brilliance, no need to worry about conventions. "If every time you sat down, you expected something great, writing would always be a great disappointment," observes Natalie Goldberg (2005, 12).

Students of all abilities, I found, began to show a willingness and, to my surprise, more enjoyment in writing; they began to take risks and discover the playfulness of writing. I no longer heard statements such as "I don't have anything to write about," and students began *asking* to freewrite. A teacher's dream come true!

Once I teach my students to write using this process, I notice that other forms of writing become less intimidating to them. They begin to approach all writing assignments with more confidence and less worry. "Freewriting is not about practicing a skill; it is about practicing the generative, pleasurable act of writing in order for students to begin to believe in the power of their words to express ideas" (Gallagher and Kittle 2018, 36–37). Eventually, we will teach students the skills they need to improve their writing further. First, we break down the barriers.

2. Learning to Write

Through the process of freewriting, students begin to write more, not only more often, but also more in quantity. As Natalie Goldberg (2005) has said, "Like running, the more you do it, the better you get at it" (11). Of course, in writing more, students give both themselves and teachers more to work with. I have discovered that I am able to use this writing to teach many, if not most, of the skills my students need to learn. I can give my students the ability to choose which freewrite they want to revise and edit. They become more engaged in the process and more willing to improve their work. Best of all, they become stronger writers in the process. "Freewriting is an exercise for making the quickest and deepest improvements in how you write. The goal is in the process, not the product" (Elbow 1998, 48). I see some immediate improvement in my students' writing when freewriting is introduced; as the year goes on, as I teach specific skills, the improvement is significant. In *Children Want to Write*, Donald Graves (2013) reminds us, "Good teaching *does* produce good writing" (21).

3. Constructing Meaning

At about the same time as I introduced freewriting in the classroom, I was learning more about the constructivist approach to learning. This is when I experienced the biggest shift of my career: *that writing is a form of thinking that can help students in every area of the curriculum.* A simple idea and yet so transformative. And I'm not talking about polished pieces of writing, such as essays and reports. Those have their place, as well. This form of writing is more reflective and spontaneous — rough around the edges.

Once I saw how freewriting could help students construct meaning, I began to use it as a form of thinking. After watching a video or engaging in debate, my students and I would freewrite for a few minutes. And, wow! The thoughts expressed on the page impressed not only me, but the students. Often, as we write down what comes to mind without censoring ourselves, we are surprised at our own thoughts. I relish the look on my students' faces when they share their writing and exclaim: "I didn't know I thought that!" or "I get it now!"

Learning to use freewriting regularly, as a process of thought, is both liberating and effective for students. Students are encouraged to formulate their ideas and opinions about topics. They will have a venue for questioning and clarifying their understanding. They will reflect. They will explore. They will learn to manage their thoughts and emotions.

4. Developing the Habit of Reading Our Work

In your experience, what do most students do when they finish writing? Nothing? Hand it in?

In my experience, most students declare they are finished without ever having read over their work. It doesn't seem to matter if it is a narrative story, a journal entry, or even a test question. They don't read it over. True?

It is helpful to teach even our youngest student writers to read over their work before declaring it finished. Because we embed this process into the routine of freewriting — "Okay writers, finish the sentence you are on, and then quietly read your writing to yourself" — the students naturally come to realize the power of reading over their work. This habit then trickles into all other areas of writing. When I then remind them to reread their work (even on a test, for instance), they understand the benefits of doing so.

Have you ever got caught sending a nonsensical text message or an email with obvious errors? I have. Sometimes I write hurriedly and don't take the time to read over what I have written. I tend to blame autocorrect when this occurs although most often it is user error! The process of freewriting teaches students to develop the habit of reading over what they have written.

5. Providing Differentiation

One of the reasons I love teaching writing is that differentiation occurs quite naturally. Expectations of both quantity and quality can easily be adjusted based on student ability levels. Really, without us saying anything, students write to their own capabilities. The process of freewriting is accessible for students on both ends of the spectrum and everyone feels good about their writing. Those students who enjoy writing are amazed at what this process does to improve their content. Those students who have typically avoided writing become more confident when they realize that they can get words on paper: four or five sentences written by a struggling writer might be a real success.

When we think of writing in various content areas, the differentiation is also quite natural. If the writing we are doing is meant as a form of thinking, again, students will respond and construct meaning according to their own abilities. Some students will dive deep and extend their thinking: analyzing, making connections, thinking critically. Others may respond more simply to the content and clarify their thinking. Regardless, our students are learning. What more can we ask?

6. Expressing What We Think and Feel

In the course of my 20-plus-year career, the biggest change I see in students is anxiety. Anxiety in children is on the rise. In our troubled world, and in this information age, it is difficult to avoid distressing news. Freewriting can become an outlet to help us sort through our thoughts and emotions and make sense of the complicated world we live in. Writing can be good for our mental health (see Chapter 11). Gallagher and Kittle (2018) would explain some of the purposes of writing to students in this way: "Sometimes we write to vent rage. Sometimes we write of something that thrills us. Sometimes we write to delve deeper into something we want to think about" (25). Regardless, the opportunity to express emotion through writing is powerful.

We began this chapter with the words of William Wordsworth: "Fill your paper with the breathings of your heart." More than other forms of writing in the classroom, freewriting assists our students in letting go, digging deep, and making connections.

Freewriting Tracking Sheet

Date Completed	Topic/Prompt	Writing Time	Comments

Pembroke Publishers © 2019 *Freewriting with Purpose* by Karen Filewych ISBN 978-1-55138-339-2

2

The Importance of Sharing

"Alone we are smart. Together we are brilliant."
— Steven Anderson

I have a niece who does not often participate in class. So say her teachers. This surprises us, her family, knowing how much she loves to talk and communicate outside of school. I know she has much insight to contribute and her classmates would benefit from hearing her thoughts. She would also benefit from voicing her ideas to help her construct meaning. It is when we have to articulate our thoughts that we are forced to organize our ideas and make some sense of them. Campbell and McMartin (2017) suggest:

> Literacy flourishes as oral language develops; oral language is the continuous vehicle and accompaniment for all literacy learning. Listening and speaking are essential for building a community of learners and for supporting literacy learners in all their diversity. (6)

Through the exchange of ideas (and not just the teacher's), our students are going to experience the greatest learning. To advance and enrich their writing, it is essential that our students share their writing with their peers and learn to contribute ideas and feedback. As Stephen R. Covey (2004) said when defining *synergy*: "The whole is greater than the sum of its parts. One plus one equals three or more" (263). By synergizing with others, sharing insights, and being open to alternative viewpoints, students can magnify their learning and ultimately improve their writing.

A Community of Learners

If writing makes us vulnerable, arguably then, sharing our writing makes us even more vulnerable. As teachers, we strive to create an environment in the classroom as safe and productive as possible. Students — *all* students — should feel comfortable letting their voices — spoken and written — be heard in our classroom community.

The sooner our students get used to sharing their writing, the better. We have all had students who share repeatedly and dominate the discussion if we let them. When establishing a community of learners, I make a concerted effort to create an environment that is fair to everyone. Yes, those students who want to read their writing aloud each time will have the opportunity to share — but not every time. Students who are more reluctant or who need encouragement will also have an opportunity to share.

All voices in our classroom deserve to be heard. We cannot assume that loud is strong and quiet is weak, or, that loud is knowledgeable and quiet is ignorant. On many occasions, students who are reluctant to contribute in class have surprised me by their thoughts and insight. We cannot assume that our students don't understand something because they don't readily volunteer to participate. We also cannot presume that they don't *want* to share. Often, they do. They just need the right environment and perhaps a little more time and encouragement. As teachers, we must set the expectations and model the acceptance of ideas. We cannot expect all our students to walk into the classroom with the confidence to share their writing or their ideas. Nor can we expect all our students to behave with inherent respect to their peers. We must deliberately create a community of learners. We must establish a climate where students can take risks, where they can share their thoughts and feelings and know that they will be respected. We must convey to the class that all members are worthy and have the right to have their voices heard.

Building Confidence

Reminding students that all of us have strengths and talents, and that some of us are naturally better at baseball, others at music, and still others at math, helps reinforce the acceptance of all despite our differences. And we shouldn't suppose that because our students are in Grade 5 or Grade 9 or Grade 12 they already know this. It is vital to establish this environment with each class, each year, as every dynamic is different. We might go about it differently depending on the grade we teach, but we cannot ignore the importance of having these conversations. They set the tone for our classroom environment.

One simple strategy I use to help set the tone and build the confidence of my students in the area of literacy is through my language. I call them "readers" and "writers" every day. "Okay, *readers*, choose your spot. We'll have 15 minutes of independent reading." "*Writers*, it's time to meet in our writing groups. Take a pencil and your favorite piece of work from last week to your meeting place." Simply by my referring to them in this way, students begin to see themselves in this way and ultimately gain confidence as readers and writers.

All, Some, or None

As mentioned in Chapter 1, be sure to leave time for sharing after freewriting. It doesn't have to be long, but the time is valuable. "You may find the reading out loud frightening, but it is crucial. For there is a deep and essential relationship between writing and the speaking voice" (Elbow 1998, 22). We write, we read our work to ourselves, and then I ask for volunteers to share their writing. For the most part, I keep this initial sharing time as simply that: sharing. I invite students to read *all*, *some*, or *none* of their writing aloud. We move from person to person with not much more than a "thanks for sharing." We do not give feedback at this time.

After everyone who wants to share has had the opportunity, we might then discuss what we noticed in the writing; however, this feedback is not given to specific writers. A sample observation might be, "Wow! Did you notice how varied our topics were today even though we all wrote using the same prompt?" Or, "I noticed that many of us wrote about our parents for this prompt." And it is not only me, as teacher, making these connections; the students do, as well. Perhaps a student comments, "Our writing was powerful today." I then ask, "What do you think made it so powerful?" Imagine the discussion to follow.

When students see and hear others sharing (and remember, they are sharing something they have just written with no time to revise or edit), they begin to realize that teachers do not expect their work to be perfect at the initial stage of writing. They also realize that their writing is not that different from the writing of those around them. Many of us — both students and adults — believe that "everyone else writes better." Through the sharing of freewrites, students begin to understand that writing is a process for all of us.

Addressing Emotion Elicited by Freewrites

Freewriting often takes us, as writers, to places we don't expect to go. This is one of the reasons I appreciate the process. In the classroom environment, we have to be prepared to deal with the emotion that may surface in our students. An "I wish" prompt might become a list of desires for a particular writer on a given day; however, it also may lead us to writing about something far more profound than "I wish for a new puppy." Through freewriting, painful topics sometimes surface — sometimes when we least expect them.

Inevitably, you will witness individual students brought to tears during or after a freewrite. The freedom of the process can unexpectedly lead our student writers to a topic that may be emotional. The simple prompt "I remember" can lead to a student writing about the death of her mother or lead another to describe ongoing abuse in the home. Sometimes, even though the topic is personal, a student decides to share this writing with the class. Ensuring that you have established a respectful, safe environment is the first step; being especially sensitive and modeling an appropriate reaction to the writing is the second step; talking with the student privately is the third step.

During a private discussion such as this, I typically give this student a journal (I always have a stash on hand from the dollar store). If the freewriting generated emotion, that student would likely benefit from continuing to express and process what is going on in his or her life through writing. The journal is not something I would expect the student to share with me. It is simply an outlet. I explain how much journal writing helped me cope with my father's illness when I was in junior high and high school. I explain, too, how I was able to express my feelings when I didn't want, or know how, to share these feelings with my family or friends. I affirm how writing continues to help me cope with the challenges of life and help me feel stronger as a person.

Writing Groups for Effective Feedback

The act of writing is thought to be a solitary process, and it is. Writing improves, however, when we share it with others to gain feedback and perspective. I know this as a writer myself but when I first brought this idea into my classroom, some of my students were hesitant to share their work for this purpose. Others were excited, of course. These students tended to enjoy sharing (and the attention it brings) in any circumstance. But students who were quieter or more introverted, or who spoke less found the idea of writing groups somewhat intimidating. Yet, I discovered, writing groups were beneficial to all students.

What became glaringly obvious was that I couldn't just let students form a group, bring some writing, and call it a "writing group." Students need to be taught the purpose of writing groups and, even more important, how to give and receive effective feedback. Once they see how writing groups benefit their work, their feedback tends to improve. Quality feedback leads to quality writing.

The Purpose of Writing Groups

For myself as a writer, feedback from a reader is not only helpful but it also spurs more thoughts and changes to my work. My mom is the most frequent reader of my writing, and her comments or notes on my page are often enough to stimulate more thought and motivate me to continue the revision process. Teaching our students to give and receive feedback in writing groups can accomplish the same purpose.

As Elbow (1998) says, "Try believing your readers: not so you are stuck with their view forever but so you can see your writing through their eyes. You are not yet trying to make up your mind about anything, you are trying to enlarge your mind" (145). This approach is difficult for even the most experienced writers and certainly something that must be taught to our students.

> **Giving and Dealing with Feedback**
>
> Professional writers know that rejection is a part of their lives: a given. For this reason, writers must become resilient simply to survive! As I was thinking about the latest rejection I received for a work of fiction, I noticed something different this time. Instead of a simple "no" or "not a good fit for our company," I received a relatively long detailed rationale for the "no." It began with some of my strengths. The editor then specifically outlined what she felt was not working with the manuscript. As disappointing as it was to get the "no," this time I felt I understood the reasons and could then determine ways to improve my manuscript. But even so, I'll tell you this … if she had jumped right into the critique without first addressing some positives, I would have found it hard to bear.
>
> Even as an adult, even knowing this industry, I still appreciate the positive comments. They encourage me to persist and frame the critique. Thankfully, our students do not have to deal with the rejection of their work, but they do have to deal with feedback. We must be careful not to bombard our students with areas to improve without first commenting on what they are doing well. Just like me, they won't want to listen to the suggestions. Giving a balance of positive and constructive feedback is important.

Depending on the length of the assignment, students benefit from feedback a couple of times during the process of revision. Once they have chosen a free-write to revise, they meet with their writing groups to read and discuss the piece they want to develop, revise, edit, and publish. After taking away this initial feedback, they work on the piece for a couple of days. Eventually, they return to their

As long as we teach our students how to participate effectively, students of all ages will benefit from writing groups.

"Talk deepens thinking and learning. Yes, there are moments when we seek deep, reflective silence in our classrooms, but these moments are balanced by the frequent buzz that occurs when students share interesting thinking with each other" (Gallagher and Kittle 2018, 16).

Writing group conversation should centre around the process of revision, not editing. Students should focus on the big ideas or the craft of writing, not the details of spelling or punctuation. There may be a time for peer editing, but it is not the purpose of the writing groups. (See Chapter 5 for more information about the distinction between revision and editing.)

writing groups to share the new and improved (but not yet final) version. This second time with their group leads to interesting discussion about the changes that have been made; it often results in more changes. Before I introduced writing groups to my students, I rarely saw my students revising their work multiple times, if at all.

Focusing on Communication and Collaboration

Writing groups not only lead to improved writing, but also help us meet objectives in the curriculum related to communication, collaboration, peer interaction, and leadership. No matter which provincial or state curriculum we look to, and no matter the grade level or even the subject area, there is a focus on both communication and collaboration. In fact, as jurisdictions have undergone curricular redesign in recent years, the focus on these areas has grown, acknowledging the increasing importance of these skills in society today.

Consider British Columbia and Ontario. In 2015, British Columbia began transitioning to its redesigned curriculum: the curriculum outlines *communication* as one of the three core competencies. A focus on communication is embedded in each discipline of study and across the grade levels. Both the process of writing and work within writing groups would meet objectives under this competency, despite the discipline of study.

The *Ontario Curriculum, Grades 1–8: Language* (2006) has oral communication listed as the first of four strands. This strand has three overall expectations.

> Students will:
> 1. listen in order to understand and respond appropriately in a variety of situations for a variety of purposes;
> 2. use speaking skills and strategies appropriately to communicate with different audiences for a variety of purposes;
> 3. reflect on and identify their strengths as listeners and speakers, areas for improvement, and the strategies they found most helpful in oral communication situations. (9–10)

Of course, it is not necessary to outline the objectives in each jurisdiction. The point is that writing groups accomplish goals in both written and oral communication regardless of the curriculum you follow: "[C]ollaboration needs to be a mainstay of the curriculum, a skill that is both used as a teaching tool and seen as a central piece of content" (Daniels, Bizar, and Zemelman 2001, 139). Writing groups accomplish this beautifully!

Writing groups are not limited to our language arts classrooms. They can be effectively incorporated into other disciplines as well. The focus could be a discussion of the content vocabulary or the style of writing specific to the discipline you teach. Or, the goal might be extending our students' learning by sharing aloud their writing about what they have learned. Regardless, writing groups are effective in many disciplines of study.

Establishing Writing Groups

I am very deliberate when establishing groups. My ideal group size is four. This size allows for everyone to have an opportunity to participate without the reading and sharing becoming overwhelming. If the group size becomes too large, students may have difficulty staying engaged the whole time. If the group size is too small, students may not feel they are receiving enough meaningful feedback. I include students of a range of abilities and personalities within each group. I try to include at least one individual who, I think, will be a natural leader and help keep the group on track, someone who can say: "Okay, let's move on. Tom, what did you notice about Bella's writing today?"

It is important that all students have an opportunity to contribute. At the beginning, we must be sure to set the expectation and hold all students accountable for contributing. With practice, it becomes the norm. If you notice a student who is not engaging and is reluctant to participate, join that writing group a few times. Be a source of encouragement for your reluctant student, model patience waiting for that individual to speak, and praise any efforts if that student contributes to the discussion.

Building Trust: It is vital that students feel safe enough to share within their group. Another reason I choose the members of the writing group, rather than letting students choose, is for an optimum productivity and comfort level between students: avoiding potential conflict and building trust. For this reason, I also keep the writing groups the same throughout the year as much as possible. The first year I introduced writing groups to my students, I did not intend to keep the groups the same throughout the year. Partway through the year when I mentioned changing the groups, my students were adamant that the groups remain the same; they had established working relationships with the peers within their groups. Now I know: once trust is established, do not change the groups unless you have to. The students taught me this and it makes perfect sense.

Considering Body Language: It is essential to teach our students how to ensure that their body language is conducive to group work. Before we begin our first writing group session, I ask students to show me inappropriate, inattentive body language — to pretend they are not at all interested in what I have to say — and then, to show me appropriate, attentive behavior. The slouching, fidgeting, heads down, snoring even, ends quickly as their backs straighten and eye contact returns. The activity is enjoyable for students, and it also gets the point across. We talk about how I, as the speaker, feel with the inattentive body language versus the attentive body language. I remind them to show they are listening attentively by making eye contact and facing the reader.

To help facilitate this, I insist that all students within a writing group sit on the same level. If they choose the floor, that's fine, but they *all* must be on the floor. If they sit on chairs, they are *all* on chairs. Doing this ensures that their body language is conducive to group work and that they can see and hear each other well. Sometimes when we let our students choose where to work, they sit all lined up against a wall or all on the same couch. While they might be comfortable this way, they cannot see each other. I remind them to sit in a close circle to create an optimal collaborative environment and minimize distractions.

Giving Feedback

I believe all students can give effective feedback. But, they must be taught. I am sure to model — not just once, but a few times — what I consider useful and appropriate feedback. This modeling and demonstration sets the expectation for what we want to see within the writing groups. I remind students that all their feedback should comment on the *writing*: elements such as word choice, sentence fluency, ideas, organization, character development, description, and the use of dialogue. As you teach various skills within your writing program, consider making an anchor chart on which you list these skills. Then, when students go into their writing groups, they can refer to the chart when thinking about what to give feedback on. Young students sometimes comment on how someone reads their work out loud (too quietly or with expression, for example), but not on the writing itself. Some students comment on the content. If they do, it is essential that they understand the boundaries: they should never question the validity of someone's work or mock someone else's ideas. Regardless of what they are commenting on, I teach them to give feedback that is *specific* and *positive*. We might be saying the same thing, but how we say it is important.

Make It Specific. Student feedback without guidance tends to be quite general: "I like your writing" or "That was really good." I share examples such as these with students and then I ask them if they think those comments would be helpful to me as a writer. No … they *might* make me feel good as a writer, but really, with those general comments I couldn't even tell if my group members were listening. Furthermore, that type of feedback does not guide me in improving my writing.

When I was guest teaching a Grade 5/6 class, one of the students read a piece she had written about rain to her writing group. Her piece begins like this: "Patter patter patter. Tap tap tap. The sounds of rain against the window, calming sounds. Reassuring almost." After she finished reading the entire piece, one of her peers in the writing group said, "I really liked the beginning of your writing because you used the sound of the rain to interest me." Now, *this* is a specific comment about the writing: beautiful! This writer would know specifically *what* she did well (used the sound of the rain as her beginning — onomatopoeia) and *why it worked* (engaged the listener). Not only is she going to keep her beginning the same, but she (as well as her group members) also knows that using words to represent sounds can be an effective technique in writing. If she had simply written, "I like rain" as her beginning sentence, we would be having an entirely different conversation. And if the group member had simply said, "I like your writing," we couldn't even be sure that he was paying attention to her piece.

Make It Positive. The first few times students meet in their groups, it can be difficult for them to give effective feedback, especially because we want the feedback to be constructive. If students want to suggest improvements to the writing, both the words and the tone of the words they use are important. Again, giving examples to students can make this clear. I tell my students that I am proud of something I've written and excited to share it with my group; then, someone says to me, "That's not any good" or even, "I don't like that part." When I ask how they think I feel, they are quick to answer: *sad, angry, embarrassed, disappointed,* and *not willing to share again.* They understand what not to say when we talk about it in a modeled situation such as this. But, we must then give them suggestions of what to say instead. Alternatives: "I was a bit confused at the beginning. Could you explain that part a little more?" or "I noticed you used the word 'good' a few times. Have you considered changing it and using more interesting words?" Not only are these examples of *specific* feedback, but they are also framed in a *positive* way. I explain that as a writer, I wouldn't be offended by these comments; rather, I would find them helpful.

Asking for Clarification
"Can you explain a little more?"
"Why do you think so?"

It also helps to discuss and perhaps even role-play what students do if they do not agree with something a peer suggests. Teaching students to listen fully to their classmates and ask for clarification if needed can assist them in truly learning from each other and being open to the suggestions of others.

Austin's Butterfly: Descriptive Feedback

To help students understand the importance and the power of feedback, I show them the video *The Story of Austin's Butterfly* featuring Ron Berger from Expeditionary Learning. Austin, a Grade 1 student, was required to do a scientific drawing of a tiger swallowtail butterfly. The video discusses how critique and descriptive feedback can significantly improve the quality of a student's work. In the video, students discuss all six drafts of Austin's drawing. Each drawing is progressively more accurate. The video demonstrates the effectiveness of descriptive feedback and helps students understand its value. Even though this video focuses on a scientific drawing, students make the connection to writing quite naturally. After watching the video, they tend to be more open about the process of writing groups with their peers.

Writing Group Prompts

To scaffold the feedback that students give to their peers, I use prompts. These prompts can be posted in the classroom or given to the students to use within their writing groups. I encourage my students to tie their feedback to something we have been learning in class. If we have been working on word choice, this would be the focus of the writing group on that day. If we have been working on leads, dialogue, or sentence length, I encourage comments specifically about these skills. As the year goes on, they have a larger repertoire of skills to comment on.

I give students a prompt page such as the one that follows to use as a reference, especially as they are getting used to giving feedback. I have laminated a set that I can give to students as they move into their groups. The prompts could also be displayed on an interactive whiteboard or posted in various parts of the classroom where students meet in their writing groups.

Writing Group Prompts

My favorite part of your writing is …
I like the way you …
Could you explain …
Have you considered …
I'd like to hear more about …
In class we've been discussing _____. I noticed that you …

Remember, stay positive and respect your peers.

Feedback Strips

As students become more comfortable interacting with their group members and giving effective feedback, I begin to use feedback strips periodically. I tailor the feedback strips based on my students' needs and often to focus on a specific skill. (Two examples of strips appear below.) As usual, students give verbal feedback to their peers. In addition, though, they write feedback guided by the prompts on the page. Each student receives as many strips as there are other members in the group.

Students then return to their desks with written thoughts and suggestions from their peers. After the writing group time, I let students work on their pieces for at least 5 to 10 minutes to think about what their peers have shared. I remind them how Austin improved his butterfly sketch each time he received feedback from his peers. If we establish this routine early on, students come to anticipate the time and will begin to realize the power of the feedback guiding revision.

What is the difference between prompt pages and feedback strips? When students are new to the idea of writing groups, I use prompt pages to guide and scaffold their conversations. They are giving oral feedback only. In time, after students have had some practice giving feedback, I sometimes give them feedback strips where they record their thoughts for their peer writers.

Name of Writer: _____ Name of Listener: _____ Date: _____

I like the sound of …

I want to hear more about …

While you read, I remembered/I felt …

Name of Writer: _____ Name of Listener: _____ Date: _____

When I listened to your writing, I noticed these strong/effective words …

I also noticed …

Have you considered …

Tell Me about Your Writing: Conferencing

The other essential form of sharing in our classrooms is conferencing. I meet with each of my students at least once a month for a short writing conference. To accommodate everyone, conferences are only about five minutes per student. Despite the short time frame, this meeting is valuable for each of my student writers on several levels: I target their learning in order to nudge them along with their writing, and, perhaps just as valuable, as writers and as people, they receive my full, committed, individual attention. Students quickly learn to appreciate this one-on-one time when they can share something they are working on. Rarely do I tell my students which piece of writing to bring to our conference. Once again, the element of choice is key. Because we write frequently, they have plenty to choose from. They are usually excited to bring something to talk about.

As outlined in *How Do I Get Them to Write?*, my previous book, the conferences often begin with the students reading me a short excerpt of something they have written. Then, we talk about the work. As much as possible, I try to keep the conversation student-driven. Students come to expect the monthly conference; therefore, they often have something specific that they want to ask or discuss. Very often, it is connected to a recent mini-lesson I have taught. If need be, I lead with an open-ended statement to initiate the conversation: *Tell me about your writing.* This is usually enough to get them talking.

Depending on the student, I may guide the conversation to a particular skill, for example, sentence fluency, organization, or writing to a target audience. This discussion may be connected to something we have been working on in class. Or, it may be an opportunity to support a struggling writer or challenge a high flyer.

I finish conferences by asking my students what goal they have for their writing during the next month. During the first few conferences, students may need support in establishing their goals. As they grow more accustomed to conversations about what good writers do, the goal-setting becomes much more natural: they learn to recognize both their strengths and areas in need of improvement.

All this information, however brief, is tracked on a line master which can help me to remember what the student and I have discussed, guide future conversations, and write comments for the student's report card. A sample line master appears on page 33.

Sharing writing is intimidating for many students, but numerous benefits are associated with doing so. Sharing our writing with each other improves the dynamics of the classroom: connecting us in unexpected ways and enabling us to learn from one another. I am often delighted or moved by the ideas students express through their writing. We often share laughter when writing is read out loud. Sometimes, we share a few tears, as well. Therefore, the time we spend establishing a safe, positive classroom climate — one in which students feel comfortable sharing — is worth the effort. We model respectful interactions and scaffold literate conversations, all in an effort to improve student writing.

My writing conferences are a set, dedicated time for each student. Of course, I often talk to my students informally about their writing.

Student–Teacher Conference Notes

Student Name:			
Date	**Teacher Initiated**	**Student Concerns**	**Student Goal**
September _____			
October _____			
November _____			
December _____			
January _____			
February _____			
March _____			
April _____			
May _____			
June _____			

Pembroke Publishers © 2019 *Freewriting with Purpose* by Karen Filewych ISBN 978-1-55138-339-2

3

Freewriting Prompts

> *"No tears in the writer, no tears in the reader.*
> *No surprise in the writer, no surprise in the reader."*
> — Robert Frost

Throughout the book, you will learn ways to integrate freewriting into the various subject areas you teach. This chapter provides a quick reference to prompts that are effective in any subject area, especially as you and your students become more familiar with freewriting. These prompts are typically universal, enabling each student to find success.

General Prompts, Varied Responses

Everyone can respond to the prompt "I feel …," for example, because we all feel something. Everyone can respond to the prompt "I need …," again, because we all need something. We are not dictating what our students write: they are going to write what comes to mind based on the few words we give them. The writing will therefore be wonderfully varied. Writing assignments on a given topic such as a summer vacation limit our students' choices and, therefore, the level of engagement. Not all students want to write about their summer vacations. Freewriting prompts, however, can lead us anywhere!

Provide a two- or three-word prompt regardless of the circumstance. Here is a basic list of effective prompts focused on *I*:

I remember …	I want …	I like to …
I am …	I need …	Today I …
I am not …	I think …	I believe …
I am from …	I feel …	I enjoy …
I've lost …	I collect …	
I wish …	I wonder …	

Some prompts, such as these, are slightly longer or written in a different format:

I am grateful for …	The trouble with …
I want to be …	I wish my parents knew …
I'm worried about …	I wish my teacher knew …
I'm not happy about …	I wish I knew …
I'm upset about …	I feel good when …
I am sorry that …	A friend is …

I am a friend to …

Everybody should …

Sometimes I dream …

Maybe one day …

I don't like people who …

What I like best about this class is …

The funniest thing I ever saw …

I'm proud of myself when …

When I was six …

The best laugh I've heard is …

You won't believe this, but …

The weather outside …

Currently I see …

Currently I feel …

The truth is …

I am obsessed with …

When we went to …

Writing is …

I said goodbye to …

I wish I had a key to …

My hands …

It's not fair that …

Learning to drive will be …

When I am older …

Let students write on a person of your choice or theirs: "My mom …," "My dad …," "My sister …," "My brother …," "My grandmother …," "My uncle …," "My neighbor …," "My dentist …," "My teacher …," "My family is …"

Invite students to write about favorites: "My favorite animal is …," "My favorite color is …," "My favorite shoes are …," "My favorite movie is …"

Choose a word, either concrete or abstract, to write about:

Love is …	Christmas is …	School is …
Hope is …	Summer is …	Home is …
Happiness is …	Money is …	
Sadness is …	Pain is …	

Put a provocative statement on the board, for example, "Every school should hire a police officer" or "Dogs are better than cats." Have students address the topic, responding with "I agree …" or "I disagree …"

Invite students to complete the following sentence and write about it further: "There are not enough _____ in the world. I think …"

Provide a sensory writing experience. The students can write about popcorn while watching and listening to it pop, while smelling it, and perhaps even while tasting it. "Popcorn is …"

Give an *If* prompt. For example: "If children ruled the world …," "If I could fly …," "If I were the principal …," "If my dog could talk …," "If I had a magic wand …," "If we ran out of water …," "If I had to move next week …," "If I could buy anything …," "If I could choose another name, I'd choose …," "If I could go anywhere in the world …"

Once your class becomes familiar with the idea of freewrites, offer a visual prompt. To prepare, collect interesting pictures or items. You could show your older students a dramatic news photo. For younger students, present something intriguing or perhaps a tad bizarre. Artwork, a wonderful option, too, is discussed more fully in Chapter 10.

Arrange for students to write to music. Try Vivaldi, Mozart, or Handel. Try Oscar Peterson, *The Phantom of the Opera*, or Enya. Afterwards, discuss the differences in the students' writing process and product when they write to music. This exercise is especially effective with simple two-word prompts such as "I feel …," "I need …," "I think …," "I remember …," or "I am …" (Music is discussed more fully in Chapter 10.)

For an interesting twist, have the class write two freewrite opposites one after the other. For example, spend about seven minutes writing "I'm afraid of …" and then surprise the students and have them spend as much time again responding to "I'm not afraid of …" Other pairs of prompts that work well include "I want …" and "I need …"; "I love …" and "I hate …"; "I know …" and "I don't know …"; "I've found …" and "I've lost …"; "My favorite food …" and "My least favorite food …"

Let students write about a sport, perhaps baseball, basketball, hockey, dance, fencing, football, rugby, swimming, diving, tennis, soccer, wrestling, volleyball, or water polo. "Baseball is …"

Choose (or let students choose) a color to write about: "Red is …"; "Black is …"; "Blue makes me feel …"

Use the change of seasons as a prompt: "Fall is …"; "Winter is …"; "My favorite thing about spring is …"; "This summer I plan to …"

Invite students to write about even the simplest of things: a blade of grass, the leaves turning from green to yellow, a vase of flowers, a glass of milk, their desks, a comfortable chair. Although seemingly mundane, these topics can yield fascinating, creative work. Again, be sure that there is a prompt and understand that less writing may be generated from a prompt like this: "A blade of grass …" or "A glass of milk …"

You might challenge students to change their point of view. They could write as if an animal: the family pet, a circus lion, a wild horse. "Today I …" or "If only …"

Prompts in Response to Quotations

As you have probably gathered, I am a lover of words. In my classroom, there is a different quotation on the board every day. I notice many students reading it as soon as they enter the room. Often, I don't do anything with the quotations: they simply provide inspiration or provoke thought, the words resonating with my students throughout the day. I encourage you to feature quotations, too.

The language of some of the quotations may at first seem out of reach for your students; however, you may be surprised at how soon they learn to grapple with the style of the language of various eras. They will learn about and from notable leaders, educators, authors, actors, scientists, theorists, and philanthropists of the past and present.

In addition to learning about various topics and people, quotations are often chosen because they are well written. Fletcher (1996) says, "I've learned that if I am going to write well, I need to surround my words with the beautiful writing of others" (108). The repeated exposure to quotations could potentially enhance the depth of students' thinking and the quality of their writing. Students unconsciously, and sometimes consciously, learn new vocabulary or emulate a certain rhythm or cadence of a writer.

On occasion, my students and I freewrite about the quotation. As mentioned in *How Do I Get Them to Write?* I also invite students to respond in their visual journals from time to time. Consider making this a weekly routine. Perhaps each Tuesday when they enter the room, they could respond to the day's quotation. Or perhaps, you could build this into Friday's routine for the last 15 minutes of class. Do whatever works in your schedule. As they write, reflect, and discuss, students will learn from each other and internalize some of the wisdom of the ages. This practice is effective no matter the age of your students.

Eventually, your students may ask if they can put their favorite quotations on the whiteboard as well. Or, if you choose a star student every week, you could make selecting a quotation one of the student's duties. Often, students get their

You'll notice that, when possible, I have indicated the author of the quotation with a simple description and the years of birth and death, if applicable. Depending on the age of your students, this detail can add to their learning and discussion as they appreciate the quotation's context.

parents involved in this search which may lead to wonderful discussion and learning as a family.

Some quotations to get you started:

- "I never lose. I either win or learn."
  — Nelson Mandela, *first South African president (1918–2013)*
- "Whatever you are, be a good one."
  — Abraham Lincoln, *16th president of the United States (1809–65)*
- "I do believe something magical can happen when you read a good book."
  — J. K. Rowling, *British novelist (1965–)*
- "Alone we can do so little; together we can do so much."
  — Helen Keller, *American author and political activist (1880–1968)*
- "Storms make trees take deeper roots."
  — Dolly Parton, *American country music singer and songwriter (1946–)*
- "Some people feel the rain. Other people just get wet."
  — Bob Marley, *Jamaican singer and songwriter (1945–81)*
- "In this life we cannot do great things. We can only do small things with great love."
  — Mother Teresa, *Saint Teresa of Calcutta (1910–97)*
- "I am careful not to confuse excellence with perfection. Excellence, I can reach for; perfection is God's business."
  — Michael J. Fox, *Canadian-American actor, author, and activist (1961–)*
- "We need never be ashamed of our tears." (*Great Expectations*)
  — Charles Dickens, *English novelist (1812–70)*
- "There are only two ways to live your life. One is as though nothing is a miracle. The other is as though everything is a miracle."
  — Albert Einstein, *German-born physicist (1879–1955)*
- "We lose ourselves in books; we find ourselves there too."
  — Author unknown
- "Never doubt that a small group of thoughtful citizens can change the world. Indeed, it is the only thing that ever has."
  — Margaret Mead, *American cultural anthropologist (1901–78)*
- "To the world, you may be just one person; but to one person, you may be the world."
  — Josephine Billings, *American volunteer and advocate (1907–2002)*
- "Give a man a fish, you feed him for the day; teach him how to fish, you feed him for a lifetime."
  — Lao Tzu, *Chinese philosopher (born 604 BCE)*
- "The most wasted of all days is one without laughter."
  — e. e. Cummings, *American poet (1894–1962)*
- "Anything is possible if you try."
  — Terry Fox, *Canadian athlete, humanitarian (1958–81)*
- "Listen, or your tongue will keep you deaf."
  — Native American proverb
- "You miss 100% of the shots you don't take."
  — Wayne Gretzky, *Canadian professional hockey player and coach (1961–)*
- "Kindness is a language that the deaf can hear and the blind can see."
  — Mark Twain, *American writer (1835–1910)*
- "The pen is mightier than the sword."
  — Edward Bulwer Lytton, *English author (1803–73)*

When freewriting about a quotation, teach students to record the quotation and source at the top of their page. They can then use one of these prompts when responding: "I think …," "I feel …," "In my opinion …," or even, "These words …"

Prompts for Reflection and Goal-Setting

Freewriting is an effective tool for reflection and goal-setting. If we train our students to use it regularly, it can be a process that leads to introspection. Curricular objectives often include metacognition: students *thinking about their thinking*. Freewriting facilitates this beautifully.

- At the beginning of a unit, students can freewrite about what they know or hope to accomplish or learn. At the beginning of a unit on magnets, for example, simply use the prompt "Magnets …" You could also add these prompts on the board for the students to continue their writing: "I wonder …" or "I think …"
- At the end of a unit or term, students can freewrite as a means of reflection, goal-setting, and self-assessment: "In this unit, I learned …" or "I was surprised by …"
- At the end of each month, have students freewrite about the month: "September was …," "In October I learned …," or "The best parts of November were …"

An effective end-of-term activity is to invite students to spend a half-hour or so rereading the last few months of their freewrites. Typically, there is a hush in the room punctuated by the turning of pages. Sometimes there is the odd laugh or two, and sometimes, even a few tears. Students are almost always surprised at how much they have written. They often begin to feel more confident about their writing abilities.

There are several things you could do with these rereading sessions.

- As students are reading, ask them to highlight favorite sentences. (Young students tend to over-highlight. You may need to say, "In all of your writing, I want you to pick your five or six favorite sentences." Students can then create a poem using phrases from their work: a *found poem* about the term.
- Students can choose their favorite piece from the term and revise and edit this piece for publication. Perhaps this piece could be shared at a parent-teacher-student conference or demonstration of learning. Or, it could be put on the bulletin board.
- One way to push students to make connections and be more introspective is by tying together several pieces of their work. As they are rereading their freewriting, encourage them to look for a common thread or theme in four or five pieces. Once they have chosen their theme (and the relevant pieces of writing that contributed to this theme), the students can meet with their writing groups to discuss a culminating project. I give students some freedom to decide how they can make this work, but the assignment is to write some introductory sentences, polish their chosen pieces, and unify them in some way. Through an assignment such as this, students will learn more about themselves and the world around them. This project can be assessed since students are given time to revise and edit their work.

Freewriting for English Language Learners

Freewriting generally works well with all students, including those learning the English language.

We must be cognizant of our expectations, however. We cannot expect a Spanish-speaking student, new to the English language, to write nearly the same amount as our English-speaking students. We cannot expect these students new to English to write as fluently, either. Increased quantity and improved quality will come in time.

To support our English language learners, consider these alternatives:

- Give students the option of freewriting in their first language. This will help them become comfortable with the process and perhaps feel more immediately successful. Even though you cannot read their writing, likely, they will be very proud to read it to you in their first language and then translate the main idea.
- Include the word *because* in your prompt: "I am happy because …"; "I am worried because …"; "Today is an amazing day because …" The addition of this simple word may help your English language learners structure both their thoughts and their writing.
- Provide extra time for their freewriting. I would be quite overwhelmed to write in another language and I imagine it would be slow-going at first! Perhaps your English language learners will want to continue writing when the rest of the class begins to read over their work and share. Offer this option beforehand. Be open and explain this provision to your other students, too, so they understand why these students may choose to write a little longer.

Gathering Details and Ideas to Enrich Writing

I blog each week. I used to wonder if I would ever run out of things to say. Thankfully, it hasn't happened yet! Natalie Goldberg (2005) says,

> Writers live twice. They go along with their regular life, are as fast as anyone in the grocery store, crossing the street, getting dressed for work in the morning. But there's another part of them that they have been training. The one that lives everything a second time. That sits down and sees their life again and goes over it. Looks at the texture and details. (53)

I don't consciously go looking for things to write about; as I go about my week, an idea for my next blog usually surfaces. If it hasn't, as I look back on the week, I think about commonalities or tidbits I have overheard. Something always strikes me.

As your students begin to freewrite more, they will begin to experience the same thing. Details will seep into their writing. They will remember the dog they saw in the park or what their mom said as they were leaving for school and store the memory for their next opportunity to write. This process will become natural for many of our students, but we can also make this process more intentional.

There are two especially effective ways that we can teach our students to gather ideas: a writer's notebook and heart maps. It's not that we have to consult thi collection of ideas each time we begin a freewrite; however, the creation of one or both of these will likely heighten our students' powers of observation and, ultimately, improve their writing. I find that once I have written something in my writer's notebook, it tends to surface in future writing. As teachers, we can also make a point of asking students to reread these collections of ideas every so often.

A Writer's Notebook

Ralph Fletcher's book, *A Writer's Notebook*, inspired me to keep my own writer's notebook even before I introduced this idea to my students. What is it? Quite simply, a collection of ideas.

> It gives you a place to write down what makes you angry or sad or amazed, to write down what you noticed and don't want to forget, to record exactly what your grandmother whispered in your ear before she said good-bye for the last time. (Fletcher 1996, 4)

As Fletcher goes on to say, the notebook will look different for each individual. Some people include pictures; others, just words. It can be in any form: scribbler, hardcover journal, coiled notebook, or as a section in a Literacy Notebook (discussed in more detail in Chapter 4). There is no one right way. My current personal notebook is a beautiful journal I was given as a gift. In it, I date my entries and write down anything I want to remember: memories, encounters, phrases I've overheard, details I've noticed, potential lines of dialogue. Anything! As Fletcher (1996) says:

> Keeping a writer's notebook can help you be more alive to the world. It can help you develop the habit of paying attention to the little pictures and images of the world you might otherwise ignore. (46)

Since I began keeping a writer's notebook, I often notice something and immediately think about adding it to my notebook. For example, one day I saw a man walking with a banana sticking out of the back pocket of his jeans. It was an odd sight! When I got home, I added this to my writer's notebook. I didn't know if or when I might use that detail, but writing it down gave me the option.

Heart Mapping

Freewriting helps our student writers dive into the depths of their hearts. They write much more effortlessly about what matters to them, and their writing, therefore, tends to have more voice and emotion. Heart mapping can enhance this capacity of freewriting and help stimulate and collect ideas meaningful to our students. Georgia Heard introduced the idea of heart mapping in her 1999 book *Awakening the Heart*. Since then she has written *Heart Maps*, published in 2016:

> Authentic writing comes from the heart. Heart mapping gives students a chance to explore what's in their hearts and to explore how they feel, what they're passionate about, and what they deeply care about. (6)

In *Heart Maps*, Heard includes 20 templates of various topics or themes for heart maps. I typically begin with an open-ended heart map ("Blank Canvas Heart Map"), modeling and encouraging my students to include topics such as people I love (family and friends), places I love, favorite activities, favorite memories, and things that make my heart sing.

As the year goes on, my students and I make other heart maps based on the templates in Heard's book. I especially like "Small Moment Heart Maps" (which could lead to memoir writing), "First Time Heart Map," "Family Quilt Heart Map," "Gratitude Heart Map," and the "People I Admire Heart Map." To help students gather ideas, I have added a heart map titled "I Am an Expert," where students identify things they think they know a lot about: perhaps a particular sport they play or a sports team they follow, their city or country, or a specific animal or pet. By teaching students to create heart maps, we enable them to collect a wealth of ideas — ideas important to them — that could become the topic or inspiration for later writing. Sometimes, we look back through our heart maps before writing. But often, without even referring to them, students will be inspired to write about something identified on one of their heart maps.

Sample heart map

As you introduce freewriting to your class, you will find the prompts from this chapter a good place to begin. First, we get our students comfortable with the process and engage them in regular writing; then, as we will explore in the next chapter, we can use the body of work that accumulates to teach our students skills specific to the craft of writing.

4

Learning to Read like Writers

"... riveting literature influences the quality of writing that students of all ages do, especially when we teach them to notice and apply what effective authors do ..."
— Regie Routman

The beauty of freewriting is that it enables our students to get words on paper. The purposes are many. Most of our freewriting is what we call *low-stakes writing*: constructing meaning, thinking through writing, and perhaps most noteworthy, non-graded writing. It is precisely because freewriting is low-stakes that our students are more willing to put their words on paper. The understanding that they will share their writing *only if they choose* is liberating.

Freewriting becomes an opportunity for regular writing practice within our classrooms. And yes, regular writing practice improves student writing. But it isn't enough. Consider this. I get out on the golf course three or four times a season at most. If I were on the golf course every day, I would improve somewhat because of the daily practice. I would improve considerably more, however, if I had an instructor providing me with specific guidance and proper techniques. The same is true for our students and their writing: they need both daily practice *and* targeted teaching.

Now, when we're freewriting, we are simply writing. We are in the moment, not consciously using strategies to make our writing sound better. As discussed, Peter Elbow talks of separating the creative process and the critical thinking process. I tell my students to turn off their critical thinking brain during the process of freewriting to let their creative brain take over. Then, during the process of revision, we turn our critical thinking brains back on, so to speak, and we become deliberate in experimenting with the strategies and techniques we have learned. We begin to practise what good writers do.

When our students read, they read the words on a page without giving much thought to how they got there. In fact, the same is true for adults. Teaching students that the words on the page were put there deliberately — *specific words in specific combinations with a specific intent* — helps them realize that they, too, can write with intention. Thus, students need examples of good writing. This is where mentor texts enter the picture.

Choosing Mentor Texts

Strong pedagogy reminds us that we should read out loud to our students daily. For many reasons, of course. But if we want them to *read like writers*, it is especially important to use quality writing samples. The good news? Your bookshelves are likely lined with exemplars of effective writing. The picture books, poetry, novels, and nonfiction books on our shelves become our mentor texts, our teaching tools. For our older students, we can also consider other forms of writing as mentor texts: articles, website content, reviews, and critiques. "When the goal is to develop proficient, confident, joyful readers and writers, it's all about texts — the quality and quantity of meaningful, interesting texts that students can access" (Routman 2014, 95). The texts we choose are important.

The Value of Picture Books

Regardless of the grade or age level of students, picture books are my favorite mentor texts to highlight and discuss strong writing: they are relatively short and easy to integrate into our mini-lessons. You can find mentor text ideas in my first book, *How Do I Get Them to Write?* Beyond that, Lynne R. Dorfman and Rose Cappelli provide many options in *Mentor Texts: Teaching Writing through Children's Literature, K–6*.

Keep in mind, though, these lists cannot possibly keep up to the picture books being published. Each time you purchase a new book, examine it for its potential use in your classroom. When I determine an appropriate use of the book as a mentor text, I put a sticky note in the front of the book to remind me of what it can be used to teach.

Consider *The Big Umbrella* by Amy June Bates and Juniper Bates, a beautiful book about inclusion and kindness. In addition to using it as an enjoyable read-aloud, I examined it to see what skill it could be used to teach. I noticed that the authors use deliberate paired repetition of sentence beginnings. I jotted this on a sticky note on the inside cover for future reference. Other than the beginning and end sentences of the book, the sentences in the middle begin in this way: "It is …," "It is …," "It likes …," "It likes …," "It loves to …," "It loves to …," "It doesn't matter …," and "It doesn't matter …" Although simple words and a simple structure, this deliberate repetition can become a discussion point for our students. "Do you like the sound of this book? Does this repetition work? Would it work for everything we write?" Even though this is an unassuming book with little text, when approached with intention, it is an effective writing example and can spark discussion for students of all ages.

When I *first* have conversations with students about what good writers do, I find they often don't realize that the authors intentionally use techniques to make their writing better. Once they realize this, they also understand that they can use the same techniques in their own writing. As Ritchhart, Church, and Morrison (2011) suggest, "When we learn anything, we rely on models" (29). They go on to say,

> Imagine aspiring to be a great dancer without ever having seen great dancing. The novice imitates experts in an ever-advancing series of approximations of excellence, learning what works best for him- or herself along the way. (Ritchhart, Church, and Morrison 2011, 29)

As busy as you are, I suggest taking a chunk of time (during the summer even) to explore the picture books on your shelves. Look at them with new eyes. With your sticky notes handy, jot down short notes for yourself, indicating what skill the book could be used to teach. Of course, this task becomes more enjoyable and more productive when we do it with colleagues!

Exploring Good Writing

Exploring and planning with mentor texts helps us to become more intentional in what we teach. Students then become more intentional in how they choose and combine their words on the page. To make the process manageable for students, I narrow my teaching focus to something quite small. For example, we study how authors vary their sentence length for impact. Students then realize that if authors can choose to vary their sentence length, so can they.

Sometimes, before I begin reading a mentor text aloud, I ask my students to think about, look for, or listen for something specific while I'm reading. Other times, we read and enjoy the book first and then look for specific elements together. Regardless, I have chosen the book deliberately for the skill I am teaching.

Often, in addition to reading the entire book to my students, I put a page or passage from the book on the interactive whiteboard to allow for further examination. I will also use the whiteboard to show passages from other books. Showing and discussing two or three quality examples will illustrate patterns, similarities, and differences within the technique.

A Sample Lesson on Word Choice

As an example of teaching our students to *read like writers*, let's consider a lesson on word choice. To begin, I read *The Fantastic Flying Books of Mr. Morris Lessmore* by William Joyce. Students listen and enjoy the story. Then, as I read the book (or a portion of it) a second time, my students are given the task of writing down some of the interesting words they notice. They do not have to worry about spelling them correctly, but I want them to make note of the author's interesting choice of words: *scattered, happenstance, drifting, festive squadron,* and *fluttering,* to name just a few. Students then turn and share their words with a partner before the whole class discusses them. Listening in on this sharing between partners, I will already begin to hear discussion and predictions about the use and possible meanings of these unfamiliar words.

After students have had the opportunity to share their words (and add to their lists) with their partners, they can share their words with the whole group. I write the words on the whiteboard as students say them so they can see them as well as hear them. On many occasions, this process naturally leads to a discussion about compound words, prefixes, or suffixes as we try to spell the words together. After the class generates this list of interesting words used by Joyce, I show my students a page or two of the book on the interactive whiteboard so we can talk about the words further, perhaps underline combinations of words, and discuss their context, placement, or purpose.

Books such as *Deep Underwater* by Irene Luxbacher and *Come On, Rain* by Karen Hesse are excellent complementary texts to *The Fantastic Flying Books of*

There is no need to read the entire book when it is used for a mini-lesson; however, students often want to hear the book once they have seen a sampling of it. So, even if it doesn't work during the lesson itself, I try to save time to read the whole book later that day or week.

Mr. Morris Lessmore. Although they are all wonderful examples of word choice, they are quite different in style. One page of *Deep Underwater* reads:

> Deep underwater, tentacles, antennae and teeth disappear into darkness …
> and an abyss becomes a bottomless pit of possibilities …

In *Come On, Rain*:

> We twirl and sway them, tromping through puddles, romping and reeling in
> the moisty green air.

Each mentor text on its own has something to teach our students. For example, in the excerpt I have included from *Deep Underwater*, I want my students to understand that use of the words *disappear* and *darkness*, both starting with the letter *d*, and the words *pit* and *possibilities*, both starting with the letter *p*, are deliberate on the part of the author. We talk about how the words sound together and how the sentences might sound different if the author had chosen other words. For example, what if Irene Luxbacher had used *hole* instead of *pit*?

> … and an abyss becomes a bottomless hole of possibilities …
> *versus*
> … and an abyss becomes a bottomless pit of possibilities …

Students quickly recognize that the second sentence *sounds* better. When thinking about word choice, they often think of words in isolation. As in this example, though, we can help them see how words deliberately chosen in combination with each other can have an even greater impact; this naturally leads to a discussion about techniques such as alliteration, rhythm, and rhyme. Students might also notice the use of the words *abyss*, *becomes*, and *bottomless*. Although the word *abyss* does not begin with the letter *b*, it certainly contributes to the alliteration (and, therefore, the impact) in that sentence. Then, looking at the excerpt from *Come On, Rain*, students might notice the use of the words *tromping* and *romping*. In this example, it is not the letter, blend, or digraph that is repeated; the author has used words that rhyme to create a similar impact.

As you can see, when multiple mentor texts or excerpts are discussed together, students begin to make connections and observations they might not otherwise make. Our goal is to help students understand how word choice can affect the sound of the overall text, create mood and style, and even help to establish setting and character. For example, in *The Fantastic Flying Books of Mr. Morris Lessmore*, words and phrases such as *happenstance*, *lovely*, *squadron*, *extraordinary*, *all in all*, and *satisfaction* work together to establish a somewhat proper tone in the book. In *Come On, Rain*, the words chosen — *mamma*, *streamers of stockings*, *phonograph* — help to give a sense of the characters, their location, and the time period.

Even though these mentor texts are picture books, our discussion can assist students in understanding how word choice is relevant no matter the genre or type of text. Most students do not recognize specific techniques used by the authors unless we draw attention to them through use of mentor texts. So, how do we know our students understand the impact of word choice (or any skill for that matter)? They begin to *play with language* during revision!

Opportunities Offered by Excerpts

As mentioned, at times I use excerpts from books instead of the whole text. Sometimes I do this in the interest of time. Sometimes the content of the complete text is too difficult for our young students. Sometimes I just want to highlight something on a specific page.

Eve Bunting's books contain many examples of effective writing, but their content is sometimes too challenging for our youngest students. In these situations, we can choose a page to highlight a technique without reading the whole text.

Another opportunity to use excerpts is during a mini-lesson on effective beginnings. As you can see by the titles of the works listed below, many of the texts are too complex and, in some cases, the content not appropriate for young students. Regardless of whether we read the whole book, examining these famous first lines is an effective endeavor.

"Where's Papa going with that ax?" said Fern to her mother as they were setting the table for breakfast. (E. B. White, *Charlotte's Web*)

It was a bright cold day in April, and the clocks were striking thirteen. (George Orwell, *1984*)

It was the best of times, it was the worst of times … (Charles Dickens, *A Tale of Two Cities*)

All children, except one, grow up. (J. M. Barrie, *Peter Pan*)

There was no possibility of taking a walk that day. (Charlotte Bronte, *Jane Eyre*)

Students enjoy talking about why they like (or do not like) these opening lines, what might intrigue them to keep reading, and what strategies they think the authors have used.

Reading with Intent

It is important for our students to understand that we read for various purposes and we read differently depending on our purpose. Typically, when I am reading fiction, I read for enjoyment. When I am reading for research, I may first skim the nonfiction resource and then if I find something relevant to what I'm doing, I go back and read more deeply. I also read like a writer, paying specific attention to what authors do: the craft of writing. Ultimately, we want our students to understand the many purposes of reading. For them to become better writers, we want them to *read like writers* — to read with intent — to be cognizant of what the author is doing.

During a Mini-lesson

By reading and studying mentor texts together, we model the skill of reading like writers. Then, as a way of gradually releasing responsibility, and to help them practise this skill more independently, I ask my students to read like writers, to read with intent, during a mini-lesson. For example, if I'm teaching a lesson on dialogue and dialogue tags, I might ask the students to open the novel they have on their desk and find an example of a dialogue tag at the beginning of a sentence, one in the middle of a sentence, and one at the end of a sentence. At this point they are only skimming the text, not reading for content. They flag examples of dialogue tags as they find them and then share with either the whole class or their writing groups. Because this exercise occurs within the context of a mini-lesson, I can provide support for those who find the task challenging.

During Independent Reading Time

Teach your students to *read like writers*.

Sometimes, I encourage my students to read like writers during their independent reading time. I might remind them of a recent lesson and ask them to notice if the author has used the strategy we have been discussing. After our lesson on word choice, for example, students might jot down or flag interesting words or combinations of words. Be sure to save time for them to share and discuss what they noticed.

The books the students read during independent reading time, then, become mentor texts for individual students. Imagine the power of students sharing a mentor text and technique that they have found with their writing groups. They might share an example of a concept or skill already taught, or, our keen writers might make an observation about something beyond what we have discussed. If a student enjoys satire, for example, the student might share how an author creates this tone within his or her writing.

Yet I wouldn't advise directing students to read like writers every time they read independently. We still want them to read for enjoyment and understanding. What tends to happen, though, is that our students become more informed and more observant when they are reading. They become more intentional readers and, also, more intentional writers.

A Small Distinction: Keep the Author Present

When discussing a mentor text, keep the author present in the conversation. Instead of simply talking about word choice or sentence length, for example, talk about how the author has manipulated word choice and sentence length. A small distinction perhaps, but an important one: the author made deliberate decisions to create impact, and we, as writers, can do the same.

Imagine how the classroom conversations in whole class discussions, guided reading groups, writing groups, and even conferences change when we learn to read like writers. I might say to the class, "Listen to Makayla's writing. She repeated a line at the end of each section. That reminds me of what Judith Viorst did in *Alexander and the Terrible, Horrible, No Good, Very Bad Day*." Or perhaps, "I noticed that Dylan used alliteration in his sentence just like Jane Yolen did in *Owl Moon*." Students, too, begin to connect what they are doing as writers to what authors have done in the mentor texts we have read. "Remember how Jon Scieszka had the wolf narrator talk to the reader in *The True Story of the Three Little Pigs*? I'm going to try that, too." These literate conversations reveal that our students are reading like writers and writing with more intention.

Creating a Literacy Notebook

A valuable way to assist our students in becoming better readers and writers is through the creation of a Literacy Notebook. Students create their own personal anchor charts as you teach the specific skills involved in reading and writing. Visual journals are especially effective for this purpose because they have blank paper and allow for flexibility and creativity in student anchor charts. Scribblers can work well, too.

Adding tabs to the journals or scribblers to delineate the sections is also helpful. Within each of these sections, leave the number of pages between tabs that you expect to use. The tabs and sections should be created to suit your teaching style and the organization of your program; the individual elements or techniques studied will depend on the grade-level outcomes within your curriculum. Here is an example of the tabs within my students' Literacy Notebooks, a structure you may want to adopt:

Reading
I Am a Reader
Genres of Reading
Reading Strategies

Writing
Gathering Ideas
Writing Traits
Types of Writing

Word Work
Word Study
Figures of Speech

The Reading Tab

Within the *I Am a Reader* section, my students and I make our own pages for I Am a Reader (in the form of a heart map), Reading Is Everywhere (see the sample on the next page), My Reading List (an ongoing list of titles each of us wants to read), and more. In *Genres of Reading*, students make anchor charts for each genre we study, perhaps fiction, nonfiction, fairy tales, myths, memoir, and poetry. The first page of the *Reading Strategies* section is titled What Do Good Readers Do? As we study various strategies, we add a sentence to the page, for example, *Good readers make predictions.* We then create an anchor chart for the strategy of making predictions. On a subsequent day, we add this sentence to the first page: *Good readers make connections.* We then make an anchor chart for this strategy. The addition of these personal anchor charts has enhanced my students' learning of the concepts. We return to these pages regularly.

The Writing Tab

Consider, as an example, how you might handle the *Gathering Ideas* section, under Writing. I tend to leave at least five or six pages for this section, where my students will create the following:

- A Collection of Ideas (inspired by Ralph Fletcher's *A Writer's Notebook*; see page 41)
- I Am an Expert (created as a heart map; see page 42)
- Small Moments (created as a heart map; see page 42)
- Places I Love (another heart map; see sample next page)

Once students understand the purpose of this section, they sometimes begin suggesting ways of gathering ideas for writing through a specific heart map or otherwise.

Within Writing, the *Writing Traits* section is where our students create an anchor chart for each of the traits as we teach them throughout the year: Ideas, Organization, Voice, Word Choice, Sentence Fluency, and Conventions. When I teach these traits, I use Ruth Culham's student-friendly scoring guides in *6+1 Traits of Writing: The Complete Guide, Grades 3 and Up* as a guideline for my students' anchor charts. These scoring guides help students to focus on the important elements within each trait. The students' charts do not have to be started and completed in one day; your students will return to them as you teach additional mini-lessons.

The third section within Writing, *Types of Writing*, is where my students and I create anchor charts on specific forms of writing. For example, if my students and I are focusing on narrative writing, we may create anchor charts specific to narrative writing. If you know my first book, *How Do I Get Them to Write?*, you may be familiar with the idea of plot patterns. My students and I create an anchor chart for each plot pattern I teach. We include the components of the plot pattern and list examples of each. When we are focusing on writing persuasive text, we would create an anchor chart outlining the important features. When focusing on writing letters, again, we create an anchor chart outlining key things to remember for this form.

What Do Student-Created Anchor Charts Look Like?

Depending on the topic (and the age of your students), anchor charts may be more structured or less. For example, if focusing on the reading strategy of making predictions, I may be more prescriptive in what my students include on the page; if the anchor chart is for, say, compound words, I am more flexible about the page's layout and look. I would expect a title and the definition from everyone; then, my students can fill the page with examples of compound words as they discover them (see the example next page). For maximum effectiveness and engagement, encourage your students to create anchor chart pages in a format or style that works for them. Although you may expect certain elements to be present, avoid dictating the form or layout. Personalized anchor charts in a Literacy Notebook are much more meaningful and effective than worksheets!

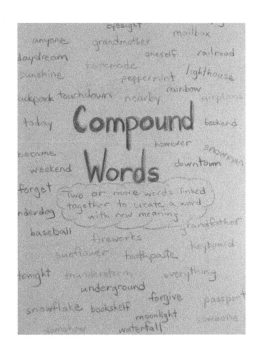

The Word Work Tab

Anaphora is defined as the deliberate repetition of the first part of a phrase or sentence to achieve an artistic effect. For example, in *A Tale of Two Cities*, Charles Dickens used anaphora in this famous passage: "It was the best of times, it was the worst of times, it was the age of wisdom, it was the age of foolishness …"

My own collection of favorite words includes *smithereens, shimmer, bliss, peace, bugaboo,* and *tizzy*.

Within Word Work, I include the sections *Word Study* (e.g., word families, silent letters, compound words, homonyms, homographs, prefixes, and suffixes) and *Figures of Speech* (e.g., alliteration, simile, metaphor, anaphora, assonance, idioms, onomatopoeia, and hyperbole). These sections are created in much the same way as those after the Reading and Writing tabs: by choosing topics applicable to the grade-level curriculum, student need, and student interest.

The first page of the *Word Study* section is inspired by *The Word Collector* by Peter H. Reynolds. My students and I give it the title My Collection of Favorite Words. Somewhere on the page, students also write *Inspired by Peter H. Reynolds*. As students encounter interesting words, words pleasing to them in some way, I encourage them to add to their page. I do the same. This page brings positive attention to words in our classroom, and we engage in regular conversation about words, their structure, and sometimes their meaning.

My students and I return to the pages of the *Word Study* section, in particular, throughout the year. Perhaps several weeks after we start an anchor chart related to a mini-lesson, my students will notice another compound word or another example of onomatopoeia while I am reading aloud. They will excitedly remind me that we should add the relevant words to our Literacy Notebooks. The ongoing nature of the anchor charts keeps conversations about mini-lesson topics alive.

Likely, as you use Literacy Notebooks from year to year, you will adjust and modify the sections and the desired anchor charts to best meet your students' needs.

Our students require the explicit teaching of specific skills to improve their writing. Teaching our students to read like writers, to examine what good writers do, is essential. The use of Literacy Notebooks can enhance our teaching, help students understand the connection between reading and writing, and provide them with a reference tool they can return to again and again.

5

Working through the Writing Process: Freewriting as Impetus

"Writing is easy. All you have to do is cross out the wrong words."
— Mark Twain

Do we *ever* take our freewriting to a polished stage? You bet! After four or five or six freewrites, my students choose one to work through the writing process into a published piece. We wouldn't want our students revising and editing everything they write. They would find it a chore and be turned off writing. Balance is key.

In some classrooms, I have noticed that *working through the writing process* means asking students to write a "good copy": a clean, neat copy. The printing may be neater, but there are few (if any) changes from the initial draft. No wonder our students tend not to enjoy the process! If the "good copy" reflects no changes to their work, they don't see the purpose of it.

To honor the practice of freewriting, I try not to dictate which piece of writing the students take through the writing process. "Choice is often the game-changer for elementary, middle school, and high school students who are not thriving as readers and writers," suggests Regie Routman (2014, 49). When we write pieces we can set aside or later ignore, we honor the *free* in freewriting. Students are much more willing to put the time and energy into the processes of revision, editing, and publishing if the writing is something they are proud of or interested in. Student choice is critical in motivating them to truly engage in the process.

Because my students and I write frequently across the curriculum, we have much to choose from. Some freewrites lend themselves more naturally to the process of revision and eventual publication than others. For example, in some of my freewrites, I move from topic to topic and my writing is less focused; in other freewrites, I dive more deeply into one topic. Our students do the same. When it comes time to choose a freewrite to revise and edit, we can teach them to choose a piece of writing that has more depth and focus; as time goes by, students become astute in recognizing which pieces are most appropriate for this purpose.

Will all of our students choose a freewrite that begins with using the same prompt or is written on the same topic? Certainly not. But really, does the content of the writing matter? Likely not, since the goal is to teach (and eventually assess) a specific skill involved in writing. Freewriting changes our students' willingness to engage in the process.

A Metaphor for Writing: The Construction of a House

The writing process is commonly known to follow these stages: prewriting, drafting, revising, editing, and publishing. To begin, let's define the stages clearly by comparing writing to the building of a house. Keep in mind that this metaphor is used to help our young students think about the stages of their writing — it is purposely simplistic. I have chosen something concrete and visual, something students can relate to and envision; however, if we were to delve deeply into the metaphor and think about it as it relates to professional writers and editors, we would find flaws.

Prewriting is commonly thought of as brainstorming or generating ideas. When taking our freewriting through the writing process, the *prewriting* stage is the task that may occur before the freewrite: it might be a discussion, a book, a video, or a field trip. Sometimes, though, we just dive straight into the drafting stage.

Freewriting as Drafting

Think of freewriting as the drafting stage in the writing process. We freewrite to get our thoughts and ideas down on paper just as an architect drafts the drawings for the design of a house. Now, we know that an architect spends much time creating precise plans and that the swift process of freewriting is not like that. The important element for our students, however, is the idea of putting ideas on paper. Once our ideas are on paper, we have something to work with and build upon.

Revision as Building

I compare the stage of revision to the building of a house: the walls go up, the roof is added, the windows and doors are chosen and installed. Construction is based on the architect's work. At this stage, when writing, we build on and expand our freewrites; we add, delete, rearrange, organize appropriately, and choose precise words in order to construct and hone the meaning and message of our writing.

Writing is messy. I have saved drafts of my work to show how many changes my work goes through. With the computer, this evolution is less easy to illustrate. But through sharing our own freewriting and crossing out text, moving paragraphs, and so on, we can show our students that our first words within a freewrite are just that: first words, a starting point, just as the architect's drawings are the starting point for the house.

Typically, the process of revision is especially elusive for students. Perhaps this is because, as teachers, we have tended to focus on editing. Many teachers have confessed to me that they skip the process of revision because they simply do not know how to approach it with their students. Beyond that, Regie Routman (2014) has noticed, "[M]any teachers focus on surface, easy-to-assess features such as mechanics, grammar, and spelling in writing" (94). Teachers are sometimes unsure of how to help students improve their writing beyond a focus on conventions. Yet revision is when the substantive work happens.

Students often think of the processes of revision and editing as one and the same. As teachers, we must be careful not to use the terms interchangeably. To help distinguish between revision and editing, think of your rubric. Typically, revision deals with the elements on the rubric *except* conventions; in a classroom context, editing tends to focus on conventions.

Editing as Making Finishing Touches

Once the structure is in place, we focus on the fine details, the finishing touches. Could we live in a house without paint, baseboards, cupboards, lighting, and window treatments? Technically, we could. But without the finishing touches, the house would be lacking in comfort and functionality. Could someone read my work before I edit it? Yes, of course, but the reader wouldn't find it as easy to do without my finishing touches. Without my paying attention to details of spelling, punctuation, capitalization, and grammar, the reader might lose the sense of what I intended and not find the writing pleasing to the eye or the ear. The reader might not only stumble on my errors but become distracted or annoyed by them.

When you talk to students about editing, be sure to suggest that editing is a way to show respect for the reader, making their reading of the text much easier. Editing also allows us to maintain a level of credibility. If we don't attend to details, if we don't consider the details important, then why should the reader believe or support our message?

Drafts of our work are generally private, shared only with those in our writing groups or others we trust as first readers; when we engage in the editing process, we are preparing to share our work publicly. These are the questions I ask my students at this stage:

- "Is this your best work?"
- "Is this work ready for an audience?"

To continue with the metaphor of the house: "Are you ready to welcome company into your home?"

Publication as Project Completion

Once we take our freewriting through the stages of revision and editing, we can create a final work, much like a finished house. At this point, we are ready for guests!

This is the stage when our students write (or keyboard) a good copy, but unlike their perception of the "good copies" described above, our students will understand why making these good copies is both natural and necessary. Students have spent time truly engaged in the processes of revision and editing. If we have done our job well, they will have made significant changes to their work. They now need to physically clean up and prepare their work for publication.

There are many ways for students to make their writing public: on the bulletin board, in a class book, as a blog post, as a letter sent to the intended recipient, as a story read to the class, and more. If we have done our job well, our students will also feel excited about preparing their work to be published.

A Structure for Teaching Skills

My teaching process has changed since I introduced freewriting into my classroom. Previously, I would teach a specific skill and then ask students to write something to practise the skill. This task was often quite difficult as they were focusing on both generating content and incorporating the new skill. I have found it much more effective to teach a skill first and then ask the students to revise a freewrite they have *already* written. Remember, through freewriting, we have separated the processes of creative and critical thinking. Once we have multiple freewrites to choose from (written using the creative process), we can focus on the critical processes at work in writing. Separating these processes and changing the order seems to simplify things for students and help them succeed at applying the techniques in their own writing.

I follow a similar, repeating pattern for teaching writing skills throughout the school year. My planning has become dependent on the structure outlined in the chart on the next page.

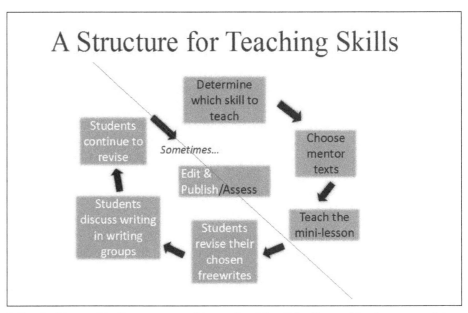

A Structure for Teaching Skills

When looking at this diagram, everything to the right of the diagonal is what we are doing as teachers. Everything to the left of the diagonal is what the students are doing. You'll notice that the middle portion of this structure occurs only some of the time.

Determine Which Skill to Teach

I begin by determining which skill I want to teach.

Let's return to a golf analogy for a moment. One morning when my spouse and I arrived for our round, we were paired up with two people unknown to us. One of them was intent on giving me advice as we golfed: *too much* advice! If someone says to me, "Loosen your grip, feet shoulder width apart, flex your knees, keep your forearm parallel to your spine, keep your head down and your eye on the ball …," I am unlikely to remember to do any of it. On the other hand, if someone says, "Keep your eye on the ball" — this, I can remember. Well, the same is true for teaching our students to write. We must target our instruction. We have to be careful not to overwhelm our students. Writing is such a complex endeavor with many components. To help our students improve, we must isolate the skills involved. Mini-lessons are an effective means to do this. The focus of the lesson should be crystal clear to our students.

How do we decide what skills to teach? Start with the elements on your rubric. Most often, I use 6 + 1 Traits of Writing (ideas and content, organization, voice, word choice, sentence fluency, presentation). These components apply to all genres of writing, and the skills can be taught and improved upon based on the initial writing of a freewrite. Choose one of the traits such as sentence fluency, a technique such as parallel structure, or a figure of speech such as hyperbole, and spend time teaching how it can improve our writing, remembering my golf example all the while.

Choose Mentor Texts

As discussed at length in Chapter 4, when we teach any of the techniques or skills to improve our writing, it is essential to examine mentor texts with our students.

Ruth Culham's 6 + 1 Traits of Writing books include kid-friendly descriptions of the traits, sample student papers, and ideas for improving the traits. I often use her ideas as a starting point.

By reading like writers, by exploring what other writers do, ultimately, we learn how to improve our own work.

I typically use a minimum of two or three mentor texts (or portions thereof) for each skill I want to teach. Examining a variety of examples assists students in seeing patterns, style, similarities, and differences. Mentor texts can take many forms; my preference, however, is picture books, no matter the grade I am teaching.

Teach the Mini-lesson

When creating a mini-lesson, it is most effective to include a *gradual release of responsibility* (Pearson and Gallagher 1983): explicit modeling, guided practice, and finally independent practice. *I do, we do, you do.* If we skip the middle stage — the guided practice — and move directly from modeling to independent practice, we may be disappointed that our students cannot transfer the skills into their own work. The scaffolded practice is important. At this stage, we will intentionally lessen our involvement as the students gain competence with the skill. At first, we will be guiding and demonstrating with the students helping us. Eventually, though, the students will practise the skill (collaboratively), and we will step back to offer support as needed.

For teaching the skills of writing, my mini-lessons often include these components:

I Do	We Do	You Do
Read one or more appropriate mentor texts.	Explore and discuss good writing samples together (mentor texts).	Students read with intention (flagging and sharing examples of the technique or skill).
Explicitly teach the technique or skill.	Examine and discuss *ineffective* examples on the interactive whiteboard.	Students examine their own writing (one of their past freewrites).
Model the technique or skill.	Work to improve the ineffective examples together.	Students revise their writing using the technique or skill.

As part of independent practice, my students choose one of their last few freewrites, then examine it based on the discussion in the lesson. Often, regardless of their age, I ask them to underline words or phrases in their freewriting as part of the mini-lesson.

For example, if working on sentence length (one component of sentence fluency), I would have students underline their sentences in alternating colors — first sentence in red, second in blue, third in red, back and forth — until they reach the end of their freewrite. This simple activity, which takes so little time, helps our students to observe their own tendencies. It also has differentiation built right in. There may be students who begin underlining with a red crayon or pen and there is no indication to stop: no punctuation! Those students must first add punctuation before they continue underlining. Other students will finish

In her books, Ruth Culham includes student-friendly scoring guides for each of the traits. The language of "long and stretchy" and "short and snappy" is from her scoring guide for sentence fluency. I use this language with students regularly. They don't forget it!

underlining one freewrite and ask to do the same to a second. Before they do, I ask them what they noticed about their own writing. One student might observe, "All my sentences are long and stretchy." Another might say, "All of mine are short and snappy." Students know from our examination of good quality writing that we want writing to include both long and stretchy and short and snappy sentences. They also know that writers intentionally use a variety of sentence lengths for effect. Often, in the examples we look at together, short and snappy sentences are used deliberately to draw attention to a particular event or detail in the story.

This same strategy of underlining our own work can be used for all genres of writing. For example, if we have examined mentor texts for their use of setting, I would then ask students to read their own narrative stories looking for descriptions of setting. They would underline what they find. Often, they realize that they have not included many indications of setting; they are then eager to add more details to their narratives based on the techniques we have discovered in our mini-lessons.

Students Revise Their Chosen Freewrites

I want my students to approach revision as an opportunity to make their work the best it can be; I also want them to enjoy the process, not dread it. When we are revising freewrites, I remind them that we had only about seven minutes to produce these pieces. Time spent revising can greatly improve them.

Revision is when we play with the words on the page. This process often begins the moment our students examine their own freewriting during our mini-lesson. The time spent underlining or circling words based on the skill we are teaching leads naturally into revision as students begin to make changes to their work. They make observations about their writing and are then motivated to make improvements. Students realize that they can make deliberate decisions about the words on the page, just as all authors do. Quite a turnaround from the students who once announced "I'm done!" the moment they finished writing. We want our students to understand the power of looking back at their work during revision: to "re-see" their own words, to take a fresh look, with some distance from the time of writing.

I have encountered students over the years who are, at first, reluctant to mark up their work. Donald Graves (2013) concurs:

> Revision presents an aesthetic barrier. The reason most children erase is to preserve the appearance of the paper. This occurs even in rooms where teachers stress lining out, or drawing arrows as a revising procedure. Children erase because they want the text to be right the first time. (49)

To help students understand that writing is a process and that all writers must revise their work, I use the book *Some Writer! The Story of E. B. White* written by Melissa Sweet. For me, the power of this book comes in the pages of early handwritten drafts by E. B. White. White's first drafts of *Charlotte's Web* — a book most of them know — show obvious signs of revision and editing. These pages are an excellent visual to help students understand that professional writers spend considerable time revising and editing their work. Students realize that if we are going to improve our work, it is going to get messy! We may move things around, cross out words or entire sentences, add in new sentences.

If I notice students who are reluctant to mark revisions directly on the page, I sometimes give them the option of using sticky notes to make comments and additions. Usually though, it doesn't take long for all of them to realize that making the changes directly on the paper (which is why we double-space everything w do) is most effective. That way we avoid the danger of losing the sticky notes. I also teach the students to utilize the margins for their revisions.

Students Discuss Writing in Writing Groups

After our students begin revising their work, I ask them to take their work to their writing groups. For example, after our lesson on sentence length, students could share their freewriting with the red and blue underlines and discuss what they noticed about their tendencies. They then might share the changes they have already made before getting feedback and suggestions from their group.

As discussed in Chapter 2, taking the time to establish expectations for our writing groups is worthwhile. To continue the house-building analogy, setting expectations is like pouring the foundation for our home: skipping this step will make all else we do futile. Although giving specific feedback to their peers does not necessarily come naturally to students, it is a skill that can be taught. Fortunately, the more explicitly we teach techniques used by writers, the more effective our students will be in their writing groups.

> The language we use during our mini-lessons and the exploration of mentor texts will become the language our students use when discussing their own writing and the writing of their peers. The mini-lessons serve to scaffold truly literate conversations.

Students Continue to Revise

After I give them time in their writing groups, I provide my students with an opportunity to make more changes to their work based on the feedback of their peers. Most of the time, I ask my students to meet in their writing groups somewhere other than their regular desk or table spot. Simply by the nature of collaboration, not all groups will finish at the same time. I set the expectation that when they are finished in their writing group, they are to return to their own spots to continue revising their work. I build this step right into the process, so they understand the benefits of *doing something* with the feedback of their peers.

If they see revising as a process to make their work better and can choose *what* to revise, students tend to be excited about the process rather than intimidated or indifferent. Sometimes, I stop after this step. Sometimes, this exploration and manipulation of our writing is enough for our students to practise the skill, and there is no need to take our writing through to publication.

> Many teachers have shared with me that students have a difficult time with editing; however, the editing our students are asked to do is often disconnected and irrelevant. Although *daily edits* are used with good intentions, usually the texts are not the students' own work and the products will not be shared with anyone. Editing needs to be relevant to students' writing for them to feel encouraged to practise the skill.

Students Sometimes Edit and Publish

The process of editing involves proofreading revised text for errors, as in spelling and punctuation, and then creating clean copy. The editing process becomes meaningful to students when they edit only those pieces that will be published or shared in some way. Students tend to care about this editing and, therefore, better attend to the mistakes on the page. They want to share their best work. Another benefit of students editing only some of their pieces is that they gain distance from their work: typically, they do not edit a piece of writing on the same day they write it.

Read to the Wall: The most effective method I have discovered for student editing is *read to the wall*. I want my students to understand the value of reading their work out loud. As Trimble (1975) says, "Your ear will catch much that your tired eye has missed" (12). Now, if I were to ask my students to read out loud simultaneously at their desks or tables, it would be noisy chaos at best. However, if we all stand facing the wall, pencil in hand, and read to the wall there, we can each hear our own voice without being distracted by the other voices in the room.

Students laugh nervously the first time I ask them to do this; however, they quickly realize its benefits. In fact, on many occasions I have had students ask me if they can read to the wall. It obviously works!

Honoring Students' Time: Although we don't want (or need) to take every piece of writing to a published stage, we do want to give our students this opportunity some of the time. If they have revised and edited their work, we can honor this time and effort by giving them an audience. This audience may come in different forms: the class down the hall, students' parents, the recipient of a letter, or peers listening to them during Author's Chair in the classroom.

Assess Student Work (Sometimes)

My students know I have high expectations when they submit their work for publication and assessment. So as not to overwhelm them, though, I strive to balance the amount of assessment that occurs. When I teach a specific skill, I do not always assess the writing for all elements. If I have just taught sentence fluency, for example, then that is the skill I assess. This focus makes the assessment more manageable for me as the teacher and, also, less daunting for the students. There are certainly times that I assess student writing for all elements, but I don't feel the need to do this for every piece of writing.

I involve the students in the assessment process as much as possible. Culham's student-friendly scoring guides in the 6 + 1 Traits of Writing books are useful for this purpose. They illustrate each trait on a continuum from 1 to 5 by using an arrow. This format makes self-assessment accessible for our students. Sometimes, I take her scoring guides and break them down even further for my students. For example, organization involves many elements. If we have been focusing specifically on effective beginnings, then perhaps this is one element of organization I assess for a particular assignment. The same might be true for sentence fluency. If our focus has been on sentence length specifically, I might have my students rate themselves from 1 to 5 only on sentence length. Eventually we can bring in the other elements.

Blogging: Finding an Authentic Audience

Student blogs are becoming more and more common and can be used in any discipline of study. One benefit of using a blog with students is the authentic audience provided by the form. Students are typically more invested in the processes of revision and editing because they know their work will be read. This realization affects the time and effort they put towards their writing.

I blog every week and appreciate the form, the platform, and the interactivity it provides. I often write the first draft of my blog entry as a freewrite. Then, I revise, revise, and revise some more. The site I use records the number of times I make revisions. Showing students this feature is valuable to reinforce the idea that nothing we write is perfect the first time we write it.

When my students are blogging, they write their initial ideas in the form of a freewrite. They then go through the processes of revision and editing before

> "The secret to editing your work is simple: you need to become its reader instead of its writer."
> — Zadie Smith

posting their blog. By using freewriting as the initial brainstorm to generate ideas, students find no need to say, "I don't know what to write."

As noted earlier, freewriting is most effective pen to paper rather than on a device; however, keep in mind that students should type the freewrite after they have revised and edited their initial version. Depending on the age of your students, though, you may want to let students compose directly on the computer. The main thing is that they need to be able to separate the processes of creative and critical thinking, as discussed in the Introduction. Composing on the computer is, I have found, effective with some students but not with all.

Blogging Tips

- Before you and your students begin to write blogs, read and explore effective blogs together.
- Keep a running list of possible topics and prompts that work well for blog entries.
- Research the age restrictions of the sites you choose.
- Always protect the privacy of your students and obtain parental permission for them to blog.
- Keep blog posts relatively short.
- Teach students to read and comment on other people's blogs. After students post their own, you might stipulate that they respond to two or three other posts.
- Comment on your students' blogs. Set a goal of five comments per blog entry and keep track for yourself to ensure that you rotate through all students' blogs.
- Most important: Do not have students write and post their blog entries on the same day.

You may wonder about assessing your students' blog entries. If you want to, you could do so because you have given the students the opportunity (and expectation) to revise and edit. What are you assessing for? That depends on your goal for the assignment: perhaps clarity, evidence-based writing, a summary, sentence fluency, or making connections.

Initially, when I introduced freewriting to my class, my intention was simply to get my students writing. As Peter Elbow (1998) says, "Freewriting is the easiest way to get words on paper and the best all-around practice in writing that I know" (13). An unexpected benefit of using freewriting within the context of the classroom was that I could use this accumulating body of work to teach my students specific skills.

In the upcoming chapters, I will outline how freewriting can be used across the curriculum. This writing will help students connect to the content and construct meaning within the various disciplines.

6

Freewriting in Language Arts

"Reading is like breathing in; writing is like breathing out."
— Pam Allyn

Those of us privileged to teach language arts have an opportunity to empower our students through the work we do. We empower our students to function in the world, to communicate effectively, to broaden their perspectives, to gain insight into the experiences of others, and to learn about themselves and their place in the world. Our curriculum is a diverse, rich compilation of human stories, both real and imagined.

It is here, in language arts, that we spend most of our time teaching our students to write. We do not teach our students to write so they can successfully pass tests. We teach our students to write precisely because it is a form of empowerment: something they will use every day of their lives in some form. When we, as teachers, come with this perspective, our students will see writing as much more relevant than if we were simply preparing them for tests.

Teaching literacy is my passion. I am excited by the possibilities that present themselves in this subject area: the opportunities to read, write, talk, listen, and learn. Yet I realize that language arts — in particular, the teaching of writing — is overwhelming for many teachers. The curriculum in other subject areas tends to be more linear, easier to follow, and reinforced by textbooks to assist us in teaching the content. Not so in language arts. And, as numerous teachers have shared with me, many teachers do not consider themselves good writers or even writers at all. They are, therefore, unsure of where to begin.

This chapter will focus primarily on how our students will construct meaning through writing within the language arts curriculum. All the chapters thus far, however, are relevant to our language arts curriculum. To sum up: chapters 1, 2, and 3 get our students writing; chapters 4 and 5 support us in targeting skills to help our students learn to write more effectively. Remember the two main purposes of writing — learning to write and constructing meaning — often go hand in hand.

What do we do with our freewrites in language arts?

In this chapter, let's explore various uses of freewriting within the language arts classroom: regular writing practice, a warm-up for other writing, reader response, and personal narratives and memoir. We have already discussed when and how we might take a piece of freewriting to a published level in Chapter 5.

Regular Writing Practice

By writing more regularly, without the pressures of assessment or forced sharing, our students will change their attitudes towards writing considerably. As Peter Elbow (1998) says, "Frequent freewriting exercises help you learn simply to *get on with it* and not be held back by worries about whether these words are good words or the right words" (14). After seeing how much they can write during a short freewrite session, students no longer worry "I don't know where to start," "this is too hard," or "I have nothing to say." They gain confidence in their abilities and a greater understanding that the words on the page are first thoughts.

A Shift in Mindset

This regular writing practice, then, is valuable first and foremost for the shift in mindset of our students: something that will naturally carry over into other writing tasks. Even as I draft this, I know that my words do not have to be perfect as I first write them: I write what comes to mind knowing that I can change things later. This thought is liberating. The same becomes true for our students. During all writing assignments, there tends to be less avoidance and more writing because they understand how to get their words on paper.

Friday Freewrites

Some of the teachers with whom I have worked have introduced Friday Freewrites as regular writing practice. Students expect and look forward to freewriting on this day. They know they may freewrite on other days, as well, in other subjects or as a reader response, but this freewrite is scheduled into the regular timetable. It does not have to be connected to something else being done in class. A prompt such as "I've lost …" or "A friend is …" might be a stand-alone task. A Friday Freewrite is an effective time to use a general prompt (see Chapter 3) or to respond to a quotation you have posted.

A Warm-up for Other Writing

Most days when I sit down to write, I begin with a freewrite. I don't plan to do anything with that writing. I consider it a warm-up. Sometimes I find a gem within (a phrase, a thought, a topic, a paragraph) and later use it for a blog entry, for a story, or for something within a book. Much of the time, however, the freewrite is used just to warm up my writing muscles: to awaken my brain and creative energy. As for a class, any of the prompts listed in Chapter 3 could be used as a warm-up for other writing. Often, though, I deliberately choose a prompt that may tap into something the class is working on. The freewrite is not necessarily something we will use directly, but it is connected to our other content.

For example, before continuing work on their narrative writing, students could engage in one of the following freewrites connected to this genre of writing.

- You could give them this prompt: "My favorite fictional character is _____ because …"
- As I do, you and your students could practise generating character description and detail while looking at Norman Rockwell paintings. After some

practice orally, show another of his paintings on the interactive whiteboard. Students can then write about the painting using the prompt "I notice …"

- Taking their own main character's name as a title, students write, using the prompt "I know that …" An activity such as this helps them brainstorm information about their character. It is helpful to list categories on the board to prompt student thinking: physical description, family members, friends, favorite things, hobbies, and so on. The details generated in the freewrite might become details they weave into their stories.

When teaching setting to students, I focus on three elements: place (room, building, attraction, vehicle, city, country), conditions (weather, old or new, tidy or messy, crowded, abandoned), and time (time of day; month; season; year; era).

- If you have recently taught a lesson on setting, students could write using the prompt "I notice …" while viewing a photograph or painting on the interactive whiteboard. Look for interesting places and keep in mind, too, the conditions and time period: a kitchen, a castle, the beach, an abandoned house, a train, a city, a forest, a meadow, a farmyard, a baseball diamond. I keep paintings and photographs for setting on a Pinterest board for easy reference.

Freewriting can also be used as a warm-up before doing other forms of writing:

- If students are writing a report, I put up a related picture on the interactive whiteboard. If they are writing about weather, I may put up a picture of a blizzard or lightning storm. If they are writing about democracy, I might put up a picture of a protest. Prompts connected to pictures can be quite simple: "In this picture …," "I see …," or "I notice …"
- If they are writing a letter to their parents at the end of the term, the warm-up prompt for the freewrite might be, "I am proud of …" or "This month …"
- If they are writing a persuasive piece, the warm-up prompt could be, "The truth about …" or "I am convinced that …" or "Everyone should …"

Personal Narratives and Memoir

Perhaps you give your students the assignment of writing a personal narrative or memoir. Freewriting can assist students in delving deeply into their own lives. Completing various freewrites leading up to the assignment or even as the assignment begins can help students in formulating their ideas and deciding on a direction or format.

Depending on the age of your students, you may decide to give them a choice of two or three prompts on a given day. After all, our life experiences are vastly different. The prompt "When we moved …" can be very powerful for some students (imagine a refugee student, for example), but there might be others who have always lived in the same house. Consider focusing on one category at a time and letting students choose one prompt from the list. A particular prompt might resonate with a particular student.

Many of the prompts listed in Chapter 3 are effective for this purpose, but the prompts below are especially useful for sparking ideas for personal narratives:

- *The Past/Memories*
  I remember …
  In the old photo I have …
  When I was [pick an age] …
  If I could change one thing about my life …
  The shoes I remember most …
  My favorite toy …

- *Place*
  When we moved ...
  My favorite place ...
  My house [apartment] ...
  My first house ...
  Home is ...
  School is ...
- *People*
  My family ...
  My brother [mom, dad, sister] ...
  I look up to ...
  I admire ...
  I like when people ...
  I enjoy being with ...
  If I could have dinner with anyone in the world ...
- *The Future*
  I dream ...
  In my life, I hope ...
  I am afraid of ...
- *About Me*
  I am ...
  My name ...
  My best quality is ...
  My biggest shortcoming is ...
- *Other*
  You won't believe this but ...
  Joy is ...
  Fulfillment is ...
  I wish my family knew ...

Let students choose any family member.

It can be both fascinating and motivating to read memoirs with our students while they are learning to write in this form. For older elementary and junior high students, I especially recommend these titles: *Brown Girl Dreaming* by Jacqueline Woodson, the Young Readers Edition of *I Am Malala* by Malala Yousafzai, and *When I Was Your Age* edited by Amy Ehrlich. With our high school students, I suggest *A Long Way Gone: Memoirs of a Boy Soldier* by Ishmael Beah, *Three Little Words: A Memoir* by Ashley Rhodes-Courter, and *Small beneath the Sky: A Prairie Memoir* by Lorna Crozier.

Always read the memoirs you are thinking of sharing with your students to ensure that the content is appropriate.

Reader Response

Reader response engages our students with what they read. Instead of reading to the end of a page, or worse, to the end of a book, without thinking about what they are reading, students can both understand and relate to what they are reading (or listening to) through reader response. I quoted Pam Allyn at the beginning of this chapter: "Reading is like breathing in; writing is like breathing out." Reading on its own is certainly beneficial but writing about our reading often enhances our understanding and helps to clarify our thinking. It can also give our students a purpose for reading. Kylene Beers and Robert E. Probst (2017) suggest:

The book — or poem, or editorial, or movie, or any other text — will offer the students nothing more than a task to be completed if all they are expected to do is decode correctly, retell completely, summarize accurately. It is only when they link that text to their own experiences that the text will begin to matter, and it may then evoke more rigorous attention, reflection and analysis. (24)

They go on to say, "When the text matters to them, then we are on our way to having responsive readers" (24).

Freewriting as a Way to Engage in Reading

I have found no better way to link to students' own experiences than through freewriting: this is where the emotional connections tend to surface. This writing is not about regurgitating details but about allowing students to make connections, reflect on their lives, and perhaps alter their thinking.

Is reader response for fiction alone? Most definitely not. Routman (2014) suggests we use *riveting literature*:

By riveting literature, I mean any text — fiction, nonfiction, poetry, biography, history, science, and so on — that captures the heart and mind of the learner and serves as a springboard to developing the stamina, interest, and knowledge that can transfer to other kinds of reading. (98)

Regardless of the genre they read, I want my students to engage. In *Disrupting Thinking*, Beers and Probst (2017) talk about the idea of *fake readers*. "Fake readers pretend to read the text, feign engagement, and sometimes extract words from the text to answer questions with little thought" (16). I don't know about you, but I don't want fake readers in my classroom; I want motivated, authentically engaged readers! I want readers who enjoy reading. We need to be wary of turning students off reading with endless comprehension questions, especially written comprehension questions. If we give them 10 or 12 questions at the end of every chapter, they will not look forward to reading the book. If, however, we allow them to periodically respond through the process of freewriting, not only will their comprehension improve, but we will gain more of an opportunity to promote and preserve a love of reading.

Then, through the process of sharing their writing — if they so choose — students are also exposed to how the text affected or influenced their classmates. Vivian Gussin Paley chronicles a year of teaching Kindergarten in her book *The Girl with the Brown Crayon*. In it, she reminds us how "the reader interprets the writer." This short read, one of my favorite professional resources about classroom life, reminds us of how sincere and profound our students' conversations about books can be. Reading together is such a critical component of our classrooms at all grade levels. It cannot be stressed enough. As Daniels and Ahmed (2015) advocate, "Read-aloud is a sacred time not only for primary children, but for everyone — including big kids and adult kids" (70).

Most teachers engage in some form of reader response with their students. Even before I introduced freewriting to my classes, I had them writing in the form of a reader response. After I introduced freewriting, there was a noticeable shift in my students' ability and confidence during reader response. They no

Just as we leave the movie theatre with a desire to talk about the movie, we want our students to leave a text with the desire to talk or write about what they have read.

longer struggled to respond. They simply wrote, not worrying or overthinking the process. Their responses became less superficial and much more meaningful and reflective.

Even students as young as Kindergarten can be engaged in reader response. In fact, the younger we begin, the better. There won't be a large quantity of writing at this age, but the students can certainly respond: through pictures and emergent writing. Perhaps they are copying a word or two from the board. Perhaps they are beginning to label their pictures by sounding out words. Perhaps some of them can respond with beginning words in simple sentences. The range of their responses will vary greatly; be open to as much writing as they are able to produce. Be sure, too, to refer to their reader response as their "writing" even if their responses consist of pictures and not yet words. Eventually we will see their writing emerge.

When to Use Reader Response

In my classroom, I use reader response in three circumstances: during the read-aloud of a novel; after a read-aloud session, which can be part of a longer read-aloud over time; and after independent reading. Reader response during a read-aloud does not involve freewriting so will be noted below; the last two circumstances will be explored in greater depth in the next two sections: Freewriting after a Read-Aloud Session and Freewriting after Independent Reading.

During the Read-Aloud of a Novel: Have you ever looked around the room while you are reading a novel to your class and wondered who is listening? Sometimes, it is glaringly obvious who has "tuned out." Sometimes, it appears that our students are listening, but we cannot know for sure. To help my students connect to the novel, I encourage them to engage in reader response while I am reading. At this time, I do not expect them to write a lot. In fact, I do not want them to freewrite. During the read-aloud, my students can draw pictures and jot down words or phrases. They make connections, ask questions, and clarify their thinking.

Freewriting after a Read-Aloud Session

After I read my students an excerpt or a chapter of a novel, a picture book, or a poem, we often freewrite. The benefit of using this process as reader response is that students are trained to keep their pens or pencils moving. They cut through to real thoughts instead of saying what they think you want to hear. They understand there is no pressure to create a polished, profound piece. They know this is simply *thinking* on paper. The depth of understanding with the text improves and students tend to enjoy the process.

As much as possible, I give my students two ways to respond to the text that has been read aloud:

- *a reaction to the book*
  This story is about …
  I was surprised that …
  I like the part when …
  My favorite part …

- *a connection*
  This reminds me of …
  I feel …
  I think …

Because they are general, these two types of responses apply to most things we are reading so can be a good place to begin. Beers and Probst (2017) use what they call the Book, Head, Heart framework: "Today, as you read, think about what's in the book, what's in your head, and what's in your heart" (62). My students create an anchor chart for this framework in their Literacy Notebooks within the *I Am a Reader* section (see Chapter 4).

Reader Response throughout Longer Works

Remember: We are not assessing these freewrites; they are designed to help our students understand, question, and relate to the reading.

Freewriting as reader response can be used with any of the books that currently hold a spot on your reading list.

In elementary school, teachers often engage in read-alouds such as *Charlotte's Web* by E. B. White, *Bridge to Terabithia* by Katherine Paterson, *Word after Word after Word* by Patricia MacLachlan, *Ghost* by Jason Reynolds, *Wonder* by R. J. Palacio, or *The Giver* by Lois Lowry.

Other novels effectively used in junior high school for this process include *Home of the Brave* by Katherine Applegate, *The Skin I'm In* by Sharon G. Flake, *The Book Thief* by Markus Zusak, and *Drums, Girls, and Dangerous Pie* by Jordan Sonnenblick.

In junior high school, your class may study *The Diary of a Young Girl* by Anne Frank. Because this text is so intense and moving, freewriting can assist students as they process the content. The general prompts listed above would be effective, but you could also use something more specific to the book itself. For example, "I am the same as Anne because …" and then afterwards, "I am different from Anne because …" Or, given the circumstances that the book was written under, the prompt "I can't believe …" is especially powerful for young readers. Regardless of the book, freewriting periodically after reading a few chapters will help students process what you have read aloud, connect to details in the text, and come to a deeper understanding.

The same is true in high school, especially with complex texts. Perhaps you and your students are reading *Macbeth*. Freewriting as reader response can do wonders to assist students with comprehension throughout the play. For example, after you read aloud the soliloquy spoken by Macbeth in Act 2, Scene 1, students could respond with "I think …" or "I wonder …" Even though these starters are simple, they are effective at drawing out interesting responses, helping students comprehend the words on the page.

> Is this a dagger which I see before me,
> The handle toward my hand?
> Come, let me clutch thee.
> I have thee not, and yet I see thee still.
> Art thou not, fatal vision, sensible
> To feeling as to sight? or art thou but
> A dagger of the mind, a false creation,
> Proceeding from the heat-oppressed brain?
> …

With these more complex texts, reader response can be approached in two ways. Students could respond immediately after hearing or reading the excerpt. Or, they could first have a lively discussion about the soliloquy's meaning, considering these questions: *Did Shakespeare intend this to be a warning to Macbeth not to commit murder or a way to encourage him to go ahead with his plan? Or, does this soliloquy reveal a tormented man grappling with a moral decision?* After the discussion, they could freewrite using the prompt "I think …"

If students freewrite throughout the reading of the play, by the end they will have quite a collection of writing. Give your students time to read this collection of freewrites before they begin to write a final essay or do a project about the text. They may be able to use some of the thoughts and reactions within their freewrites as part of the larger assignment, or at least as a springboard.

Our students will benefit from freewriting regardless of whether we are reading the classics (such as *The Great Gatsby* by F. Scott Fitzgerald, *Of Mice and Men* by John Steinbeck, and *To Kill a Mockingbird* by Harper Lee) or contemporary novels (such as *American Street* by Ibi Zoboi, *Far from the Tree* by Robin Benway, and *Under the Feet of Jesus* by Helena Maria Viramontes).

Reader Response after Picture Books

Picture books are a powerful and effective medium for students of all ages. Elementary teachers are known for their collections and sometimes obsessions with picture books. (*I speak of myself here.*) Many exceptional junior high and high school teachers find ways to make use of this medium as well. In the past, picture books were designed to appeal to young audiences. The picture books published today, however, are designed for a wide range of audiences. Many, in fact, are not appropriate for our younger audiences because of the serious nature of the topics.

When we read aloud such books, freewriting will help our students process the content. For example, after sharing *Freedom Summer* by Deborah Wiles or *Don't Laugh at Me* by Steve Seskin, I sometimes put two prompts ("I am thinking about …" and "I feel …") on the board for students to choose from. They begin their freewrite with one of the prompts. If their brain stops and, therefore, their hand stops momentarily, they know they are to write the prompt again. If there are two prompts on the board, however, they are welcome to choose the second one this time. They write without stopping while making connections.

The book *The Memory Tree* by Britta Teckentrup is one that I use when a student in my class has experienced a death in the family. Depending on the situation, I might share this book with the family who has experienced the loss. But I am also sure to read this book to the class when that student is away. After my reading, we freewrite. By putting these two prompts on the board — "I am thinking about …" and "I feel …" — students often write about their classmate who has experienced loss. Thinking about the book could also lead to writing about a time when the writer experienced a loss in the family. Either way, this becomes powerful writing time.

Simply hearing picture books like these read aloud can change student perspectives, change their thought processes, and open them to other experiences. But writing about these books — with no worry or expectation of sharing our thoughts — is even more effective: thinking time, reflecting time, connecting time. If we choose to share, we do.

As evident from Chapter 4, I use picture books to teach many of the skills involved in written communication. When I am teaching these skills, the students and I examine the text closely and talk about what the author has done. Typically during a reader response, I simply give the students the opportunity to respond to the text to assist with comprehension and processing.

Regardless of the grade you teach, you will likely find that your students enjoy seeing the picture book illustrations during a read-aloud. For instance, when I use Phoebe Gilman's *Something from Nothing* as a mentor text, Grade 6 students still want to see the pictures.

Picture Books for Reader Response	
Book Title	**Author(s)**
Alexander and the Terrible, Horrible, No Good, Very Bad Day	Judith Viorst
Amazing Grace	Mary Hoffman
Beautiful Hands	Kathryn Otoshi
Beautiful Oops!	Barney Saltzberg
The Best Part of Me	Wendy Ewald
The Big Umbrella	Amy June Bates and Juniper Bates
BookSpeak! Poems about Books	Laura Purdie Salas
The Boy Who Loved Words	Roni Schotter
A Chair for My Mother	Vera B. Williams
A Child of Books	Oliver Jeffers and Sam Winston
City Dog, Country Frog	Mo Willems
Comet's Nine Lives	Jan Brett
Courage	Bernard Weber
Desmond and the Very Mean Word	Archbishop Desmond Tutu and Douglas Carlton Abrams
Dog Days of School	Kelly DiPucchio
Dream: A Tale of Wonder, Wisdom and Wishes	Susan V. Bosak
Enemy Pie	Derek Munson
For Just One Day	Laura Leuck
Goal!	Mina Javaherbin
Grandma's Scrapbook	Josephine Nobisso
Grandpa's Face	Eloise Greenfield
Hug Machine	Scott Campbell
I Can Be Anything	Jerry Spinelli
I Carry Your Heart with Me	e. e. Cummings, Mati McDonough (illustrator)
The Important Book	Margaret Wise Brown
I'm Bored	Michael Ian Black
Interrupting Chicken	David Ezra Stein
Kitchen Dance	Maurie J. Manning
The Knowing Book	Rebecca Kai Dotlich

Picture Books for Reader Response	
Book Title	**Author(s)**
Library Lion	Michelle Knudsen
Little Blue Chair	Cary Fagan
Little Red Writing	Joan Holub
The Loud Book	Deborah Underwood
The Magic Hat	Mem Fox
The Memory Tree	Britta Teckentrup
The Monsters' Monster	Patrick McDonnell
No One But You	Douglas Wood
Oh Dear, Geoffrey!	Gemma O'Neill
The OK Book	Amy Krouse Rosenthal
Old Turtle	Douglas Wood
Once upon a Northern Night	Jean E. Pendziwol
One	Kathryn Otoshi
One Green Apple	Eve Bunting
One Today	Richard Blanco
Only One You	Linda Kranz
A Perfect Day	Lane Smith
The Quiet Book	Deborah Underwood
The Raft	Jim LaMarche
Reading Makes You Feel Good	Todd Parr
The Right Word: Roget and His Thesaurus	Jen Bryant
Russell the Sheep	Rob Scotton
Shortcut	Donald Crews
Sparky	Jenny Offill
Stars	Mary Lyn Ray
Sylvester and the Magic Pebble	William Steig
Ten Cents a Pound	Nhung Tran-Davies
Thank You, Mr. Falker	Patricia Polacco
That's Not Hockey!	Andrée Poulin
This House, Once	Deborah Freedman
Town Mouse, Country Mouse	Jan Brett

Up the Creek	Nicholas Oldland
The Very Hungry Bear	Nick Bland
Virginia Wolf	Kyo Maclear
What Do You Do with an Idea?	Kobi Yamada
Will's Words: How William Shakespeare Changed the Way You Talk	Jane Sutcliffe
The Word Collector	Peter H. Reynolds
Yard Sale	Eve Bunting
Zero	Kathryn Otoshi

Many of the powerful books I use for reader response are connected to other subject areas and are therefore listed in the upcoming chapters.

Reader Response after Poetry

Most teachers of language arts or English have their favorite poems to share with students. In elementary school, it may be the poems of Shel Silverstein, Jack Prelutsky, e. e. Cummings, or Jane Yolen. In junior high school, it may be the poems of Natasha Trethewey, Sylvia Plath, Dylan Thomas, or Langston Hughes. In high school, the poetry of William Blake, Seamus Heaney, Margaret Atwood, or Emily Dickinson may appeal to students. Regardless, reading a specific poem or a collection of poems can lead to emotional, reflective writing.

One way to approach the reading of an emotionally moving poem is to deliver it quite slowly and simply — as if you are actively thinking about it as you go — your voice going down, not up, at the end of each sentence.

Poetry, especially the poetry we first share aloud with older students, is often emotionally charged and dealing with universal themes. Many students are intimidated by the poems we read, especially if we jump right into analysis. Writing about the poems can help our students connect to the content or the language before we study the poetic devices used by the writer. For example, the poem "Home" by Warsan Shire is an emotional account of the refugee crisis. It seems especially topical and provides profound insight into the lives of those who decide to flee their countries. Although Shire uses poetic devices in her writing and you may eventually study them with your students, the initial power of the poem is the emotional reaction it stirs. Writing about this poem immediately after reading or hearing it yields intense connections and powerful writing.

Freewriting after Independent Reading

Reader response can also occur after our students' independent reading time. Sometimes, I initiate a freewrite after we have all been reading independently; other times, individual students may choose to freewrite as part of their reading time. Regardless, in these situations, it is most effective for students to choose their own prompt since presumably they are all reading different texts. Post a list in the classroom or provide individual copies for students to reference.

Prompts can be used for all genres of reading though some are more suited to fiction, some to poetry, and others to nonfiction. As you can see, the prompts given below are effective for students of all ages, including adults. Though the words are simple, the responses will range widely depending on the age of the student and the content of the text. Freewriting helps our students to engage in the texts, even those that are quite complex. Most of these reader response prompts can be used in all subject areas.

I noticed …	I can't believe …
I think …	I can visualize …
I wish …	The setting of the story …
This book [character, setting] reminded me of …	I felt _____ when …
I like the way …	I learned …
I wonder why …	I was surprised that …
I relate to [pick a character] because …	This author …
I would [or wouldn't] recommend this book because …	The most interesting thing I discovered …
I was puzzled by …	While reading this book, I felt …
	This information applies to my own life because …

Author Studies: "The Books by …"

In addition to individual reader response entries, freewriting can be used to explore thoughts about a collection of books by the same author. For example, the prompt could be "The books by Lois Lowry …" If they are using a prompt such as this, students should be familiar with freewrites. Although this is where they begin, they could continue their writing using phrases such as "I think …" and "I noticed …" if they get stuck during the sustained writing time. Often, when responding to a collection of an author's books, students write about commonalities between the books, the connections they see, or even the style of writing. This freewrite could become a draft or the groundwork for a final project synthesizing or encapsulating an author's work.

Discovering Theme

Many language arts teachers plan and teach in themes. Some of my favored themes that work well with students are friendship, family, journeys, perseverance, courage, hope, identity, racism, heroism, survival, the power of words, and teamwork. Start with a favorite book, determine what you perceive to be a general theme, and then search for other books (picture books or novels) that connect.

In *Book Love: Developing Depth, Stamina, and Passion in Adolescent Readers*, Penny Kittle (2013) suggests approaching a theme through essential questions that can be explored and discussed throughout the year or during a particular unit. Consider questions such as these:

- How do others see the world differently than I do?
- How do our experiences shape our identities?
- How do I fit into the world?

When we ask our students to freewrite in response to these questions, I still find it most effective to provide a prompt that students can write and rewrite as necessary. There are two main ways to approach this. First, and perhaps most effective, the question could be written on the board for the students to see and then they are encouraged to use a simple prompt such as "I think …" or "I believe …" Or, you could carefully rephrase the question according to the texts you are using and the age of your students: "Our experiences shape our identities by …" or "I see the world the way I do because …" As you can see, there are different levels of complexity here. We want to consider what will be most effective for our own group of students.

Perhaps, instead of providing the students with the theme, we could encourage them to uncover similarities or determine a theme as they freewrite about the texts they read. I uncovered a theme when I was reading, researching, and writing during the coursework of my master's degree: words change worlds. Once I recognized this idea, it seemed to be evident in everything I read and watched. It then became the topic and title of my final project, and ultimately, it has become my company name and website. All because I was searching for a theme.

In her text on book love, Penny Kittle (2013) observes: "The amount of reading students do matters. To be engaged with the deep reading of literature, you first have to be comfortable with words, lots of them over hundreds of pages. Our students need to read dozens and dozens of books a year. Not all of these books will be classic literature, but some will be" (23). In the same vein, I would argue that the amount of writing students do matters. When students write using the process of freewriting, when teachers limit assessment and target specific skills, students will become better writers, learn more about themselves, and perhaps discover how they might contribute to the human story.

7

Freewriting in Social Studies

"Study the past if you would define the future."
— Confucius

In social studies, we learn about history, culture, communities, current events, and principles such as democracy, equality, justice, and freedom. Indeed, social studies is the study of people and the way we function in the world. When we contemplate and consider our social studies curriculums, we realize that we are ultimately teaching story: stories of the past, stories of individuals, and stories of societies. Regardless of the specific topic, social studies challenges us to understand how we fit into the world from social, geographical, and historical viewpoints. Nelson Mandela once said, "Education is the most powerful weapon which you can use to change the world." By studying, reflecting on, and discussing past events, students can develop attitudes, skills, and knowledge to help them understand the past, make sense of the world today, and construct their future. Writing is an important part of this process.

Although we typically think of teaching writing as a function of the language arts teacher, freewriting in social studies can be used to accomplish objectives and enhance our students' learning. We consider the two purposes of freewriting in the classroom: *learning to write* and *constructing meaning*.

Helping Students Learn to Write

As teachers, we know our students must learn to write. We may also realize that the teaching of writing does not occur only within the confines of the language arts classroom. If you are an elementary teacher, teaching most (if not all) subjects to your students, a cross-curricular approach and way of thinking is fairly standard. In junior high and high school, with teachers focused on specific subject areas, many social studies teachers wonder how they can possibly include the teaching of writing in their classrooms, but they can.

Although much of our literacy curriculum will be taught by the language arts teacher, there is a place for teaching the skills of writing within the social studies curriculum. For example, one skill listed in the Alberta Social Studies, Kindergarten to Grade 12 program of studies, states that students will learn to "communicate ideas and information in an informed, organized and persuasive manner." Social studies teachers, then, are expected to instruct students on how to do this: teaching skills related to clarity, effective beginnings, content vocabulary, and persuasive language. Chapters 4 and 5 assist all teachers — no matter the discipline — in helping our students *learn to write*.

Constructing Meaning

Much of the freewriting we do in social studies will help our students *construct meaning*. In order to help them understand the concepts and content they are learning, freewriting is used as a form of thinking. The Alberta Education (2015) Language Arts curriculum overview says this: "Thinking, learning and language are interrelated. From Kindergarten to Grade 12, students use language to make sense of and bring order to their world." Many social studies curriculums challenge us to teach our students to appreciate multiple perspectives, engage in the process of inquiry, demonstrate a global consciousness, think both critically and creatively, apply the skills of metacognition, and clearly communicate ideas. We do all of this through and with language. In essence, we cannot separate our learning and the language use that surrounds our learning. The two things are inextricably intertwined.

When we look at the curricular objectives and topics in social studies curriculums, it becomes evident how freewriting can enhance our students' learning from Grade 1 to Grade 12. Although the specifics of the curriculum vary from place to place, often the overall themes and ideas are similar: identity, community, citizenship, democracy, rights and freedoms, and globalization. Therefore, the suggestions provided can easily be adapted to your specific content and the age of your students. As you begin to use this process within the classroom, I expect you will find countless ways to enrich your students' learning through freewriting.

Do not feel the need *to do something* with everything students write. As already discussed, we should not assess our students' freewriting unless we have given them time to revise and edit their work. This practice does not change just because the subject has changed: the principle remains the same.

What do we do with our freewrites in social studies?

Most of our students' freewriting in social studies will exist as documentation of their thoughts at the time they expressed them, of their attempts to clarify their thinking, and of their connections to the content. As we do in language arts, students can look through their freewrites periodically and take one to a published state. This is when you as a social studies teacher can teach writing concepts such as clarity, effective beginnings, content vocabulary, and persuasive language.

If you do decide to ask students to take their writing to a published state, consider giving them an audience: their parents, another class in the school, the principal, residents in a nearby senior citizens' home, an organization, or even a government representative such as your mayor. When choosing the audience, be sure to consider the purpose of the writing. Is it a persuasive piece, a demonstration of learning, a request, an autobiography, or the story of their family ancestry? Each of these assignments could begin as a freewrite or stem from a freewrite already written.

Inspired by Literature

Regardless of the age of our students, literature can help our students understand events and stories of the people or culture we are studying. Literature is a window into lived experience. I was reminded of this when I read the novel *The Nightingale* by Kristin Hannah, set in France during the Second World War. Although I have studied history, visited museums, and read many nonfiction accounts about this war, this novel significantly enhanced my understanding of the realities of war: its impact and implications, the destruction and devastation. Facts are essential, but I found that this book of historical fiction helped me to empathize with and understand what people experienced during the war more than any statistic or textbook could do on its own. Judy Willis (2017), neurologist and teacher, explains, "Weaving learning into a story makes learning more interesting, activates the brain's positive emotional state, and hooks the information into a strong memory template."

When I was a young student, I was not good at remembering information. Subjects such as history and biology were especially painful because I perceived the need to memorize facts. Somewhere in my schooling journey, I realized that if I tried to understand and connect to the concepts, rather than memorize them, I would remember what I had learned. I remembered this lesson when I became a teacher. We do not want our students to learn facts in isolation. We want them to understand and connect to the facts on the page. As teachers, we want to breathe life into learning. Stories accomplish this beautifully.

Literature, therefore, helps our students understand an event, concept, or group of people on a deeper level; it also helps develop a sense of empathy. Michele Borba (2016) suggests, "Books can be portals to understanding other worlds and other views, to helping our children be more open to differences and cultivate new perspectives" (78–79). Is this not what social studies is all about?

In this section, I focus on using fiction to support our students' understanding of concepts; however, the use of other literature, such as newspaper articles and famous speeches, would also be effective.

A Safe Way to Encounter the Truth

For example, if we are teaching the history of the Indigenous peoples in Canada, we can use the picture book *I Am Not a Number* by Jenny Kay Dupuis and Kathy Kacer, or the graphic novels *7 Generations: A Plains Cree Saga* by David Alexander Robertson and *Secret Path* by Gord Downie, to help our students understand the experience of residential schools. These books, based on the lives of actual people, illustrate the terrible truths about this aspect of Canadian history. Students can put themselves into the experiences of characters in the books. (*Secret Path* also has audio and visual material to go with it, making it easier to share with your whole class.) Because these texts and visuals are so powerful, freewriting is a safe way for students to process the realities faced by Indigenous individuals and raise any questions or anxieties that may surface during reading or discussion. If we have Indigenous students in our classes, we must be sure to prepare them adequately for the lesson. It can be emotional for all students, but especially those who may have had family members in these situations.

Although it is important to recognize the history of the Indigenous peoples, it is also important to include books that focus on positive aspects of their lives, traditions, and cultures, such as *Go Show the World: A Celebration of Indigenous Heroes* by Wab Kinew and *When the Trees Crackle with Cold* by Bernice Johnson-Laxdal and Miriam Korner.

A Means to Connect to Curriculum Content

Freewriting about the literature we read is a powerful means to make connections to the content. The tables in the upcoming pages list options for effective literature in our social studies classrooms.

I highly recommend reading the books before use — picture books, novels, or biographies — to ensure that they are appropriate for your students.

The first table lists picture books (see pages 81 to 83). Be sure to review it even if you are not teaching at the elementary level. Sometimes junior high and high school teachers shy away from picture books, thinking they are only for the very young; however, many of these titles are not appropriate for our younger students because of the gravity of the content.

The second table features both novels and biographies (see pages 83 to 84). Although you may be concerned about taking time to read aloud a novel to your junior high or high school students during social studies class, the time will be well spent. Ten or 12 minutes at the beginning or end of a class for a few consecutive weeks: novel complete. And the rewards? Rich discussion, a deeper understanding of historical events, and ultimately, expanded minds.

In *Rethinking High School*, authors Harvey Daniels, Marilyn Bizar, and Steven Zemelman (2001) explain how a teacher, Kate Lang, approached her sophomore U.S. history class.

> … Kate integrated the use of book clubs to read biographies and novels about life in China in the 1930s, the study of statistical data to comprehend events, and other strategies usually reserved for English and math classes. Ultimately, Kate's students covered all the state-mandated subject matter about World War II, including the textbook facts and figures, but they also emerged from this thematic unit with a visceral sense of the horror of war and the complexity of its causes. (107)

These thematic approaches lend themselves to reading and writing about the subject area and, therefore, constructing meaning from the content. Rather than memorizing the facts of the Second World War, students in this classroom connected to the experiences in ways just not possible from a textbook alone.

The freewriting prompts connected to literature can be quite simple because the content of the book and the reaction of the writer will carry the writing.

I feel …	I can't imagine …
I didn't know …	I am surprised that …
I wonder …	I've realized …
I think …	

"Learning is not about memorizing. Learning is about being mindful" (Dennis Littky 2004, 10).

The words are unassuming, but they lead to powerful and sometimes profound responses by our students, simply because of the topic. Students write, I write, and sometimes … tears flow. I prepare my students for this beforehand. The responses tend to be emotional reactions to the information they are learning: if this occurs, they are truly connecting. Although I appreciate a discussion on these topics, freewriting is sure to engage all students in a response. I often have them freewrite first and then engage in a discussion afterwards. Again, it is important to note that students can share *all*, *some*, or *none* of their written responses on any given day.

Picture Books for Use in Social Studies		
Book Title	Author(s)	Topic, Themes
Alego	Ningeokuluk Teevee	Inuit life
As Fast as Words Could Fly	Pamela M. Tuck	Civil rights movement, racism
Baseball Saved Us	Ken Mochizuki	Japanese American internment, Pearl Harbor
Beatrice's Goat	Page McBrier	Human needs, African culture
Benno and the Night of Broken Glass	Meg Wiviott	Holocaust
The Boy Who Harnessed the Wind	William Kamkwamba & Bryan Mealer	Rural economic development, community
Brave Girl: Clara and the Shirtwaist Makers' Strike of 1909	Michelle Markel	Immigrants, social activism, workers' rights
The Butterfly	Patricia Polacco	Nazi occupation of France, French underground and resistance
Every Day Is Malala Day	Rosemary McCarney	Education, human rights, gender equality, freedom of speech
Four Feet, Two Sandals	Karen Lynn Williams & Khadra Mohammed	Human needs, refugees, immigration
14 Cows for America	Carmen Agra Deedy	9/11, international relations, global community
Freedom Summer	Deborah Wiles	Civil rights, identity, race
Ghost Train	Paul Yee	Immigration of the Chinese to North America
Gift Days	Kari-Lynn Winters	Education, gender equality, United Nations: Rights of the Child
Gleam and Glow	Eve Bunting	War, freedom
Go Show the World: A Celebration of Indigenous Heroes	Wab Kinew	Contributions of Canadian and American Indigenous peoples
The Harmonica	Tony Johnston	Holocaust, concentration camps
Henry's Freedom Box	Ellen Levine	Slavery, freedom
Hiawatha and the Peacemaker	Robbie Robertson	Unity among the Iroquois
I Am Not a Number	Jenny Kay Dupuis & Kathy Kacer	Residential schools, identity, government, citizenship
Islandborn	Junot Diaz	Immigration, identity, diversity
It Takes a Village	Hillary Rodham Clinton	Community
Lessons from a Street Kid	Craig Kielburger	Child labor, poverty, generosity
The Librarian of Basra	Jeanette Winter	Freedom of expression, war
The Little House	Virginia Lee Burton	Rural/urban, community

Picture Books for Use in Social Studies

Book Title	Author(s)	Topic, Themes
Little Leaders: Bold Women in Black History	Vashti Harrison	Biography, Black history, women
Little Leaders: Visionary Women around the World	Vashti Harrison	Biography, women
The Memory String	Eve Bunting	Family history
Mirror	Jeannie Baker	Comparison between two cultures: Australian and North African
Our Flag: The Story of Canada's Maple Leaf	Ann-Maureen Owens & Jane Yealland	National symbol, citizenship
Out	Angela May George	Immigration
Planting the Trees of Kenya	Claire A. Nivola	Community, using the land for sustainability, African cultures
Secret Path	Gord Downie	Residential schools
She Persisted around the World: 13 Women Who Changed History	Chelsea Clinton	Historical figures, activism
Separate Is Never Equal: Sylvia Mendez and Her Family's Fight for Desegregation	Duncan Tonatiuh	Segregation, racism
Shin-chi's Canoe	Nicola I. Campbell	Residential schools
Shi-shi-etko	Nicola I. Campbell	Residential schools
Smoky Night	Eve Bunting	Urban violence, rioting
Something Beautiful	Sharon Dennis Wyeth	Cultural diversity
Stepping Stones: A Refugee Family's Journey	Margriet Ruurs	Immigration, refugees
Stormy Seas: Stories of Young Boat Refugees	Mary Beth Leatherdale	Refugees
Terrible Things: An Allegory of the Holocaust	Eve Bunting	Holocaust
The Tree in the Courtyard: Looking through Anne Frank's Window	Jeff Gottesfeld	Holocaust
The Tower	Richard Paul Evans	Community, equality
Train to Somewhere	Eve Bunting	Homelessness, orphans, identity
Unspoken	Henry Cole	Underground Railroad
Viola Desmond Won't Be Budged!	Jody Nyasha Warner	Civil rights, biography
The Wall	Eve Bunting	Vietnam War memorial
We Planted a Tree	Diane Muldrow	Comparison between cultures

What the World Eats	Faith D'Aluisio	A photographic collection of food around the world
When We Are Alone	David Alexander Robertson	Residential schools
The Whispering Town	Jennifer Elvgren	Holocaust

Novels/Biographies for Use in Social Studies*		
Book Title	**Author(s)**	**Topic, Themes**
The Book Thief	Markus Zusak	Holocaust
The Boy in the Striped Pajamas	John Boyne	Holocaust, prejudice, racism
The Boy Who Harnessed the Wind	William Kamkwamba & Bryan Mealer	Rural economic development, community
Child Soldier: When Boys and Girls Are Used in War	Michel Chikwanine & Jessica Dee Humphreys	War, biography
The Diary of a Young Girl	Anne Frank	Holocaust
A Different Pond	Bao Phi	Immigration, family history
Elijah of Buxton	Christopher Paul Curtis	Slavery
Fever 1793	Laurie Halse Anderson	Epidemics
Ghost Boys	Jewell Parker Rhodes	Violence, racism
The Giver	Lois Lowry	Dystopian society, government
Hana's Suitcase	Karen Levine	Holocaust
Hidden Figures (Young Readers' Edition)	Margot Lee Shetterly	Biography, astronomy, space, women's rights
I Am David	Anne Holm	Concentration camps, freedom
I Am Malala	Malala Yousafzai	Memoir, education, human rights, gender equality
Irena's Children (Young Readers Edition)	Tilar J. Mazzeo (adapter: Mary Cronk Farrell)	Biography, Second World War, Holocaust
Inside Out and Back Again	Thanhha Lai	Refugees, immigration
A Long Way Gone: Memoirs of a Boy Soldier	Ishmael Beah	Biography, war
Lord of the Flies	William Golding	Civilization
My Childhood under Fire: A Sarajevo Diary	Nanja Halilbegovich	War, diary entries
Number the Stars	Lois Lowry	Holocaust
Out of the Dust	Karen Hesse	The Depression
The Red Pencil	Andrea Davis Pinkney	Refugees
Refugee	Alan Gratz	Refugees (three time periods)

Novels/Biographies for Use in Social Studies*		
Book Title	Author(s)	Topic, Themes
Salt to the Sea	Ruta Sepetys	Second World War, refugees
A Separate Peace	John Knowles	Second World War
Sit	Deborah Ellis	Social justice
A Tale of Two Cities	Charles Dickens	French Revolution
To Kill a Mockingbird	Harper Lee	Class structure, race
Ugly	Robert Hoge	Memoir
Unwind (Unwind Dystology)	Neal Shusterman	Dystopian society
Warriors Don't Cry: A Searing Memoir of the Battle to Integrate Little Rock's Central High	Melba Pattillo Beals	Racism, civil rights movement
What Was the Underground Railroad?	Yona Zeldis McDonough	Slavery, freedom
Witness	Karen Hesse	Racism, prejudice
Who Was Anne Frank?	Ann Abramson	Biography, Holocaust
Who Was Gandhi?	Dana Meachen Rau	Biography, peace, human rights
Who Was Martin Luther King, Jr.?	Bonnie Bader	Biography, civil rights
Who Was Rosa Parks?	Yona Zeldis McDonough	Biography, civil rights

*Research and read the book to determine whether it is appropriate for your students.

If you are a social studies teacher who does not also teach language arts or English to your students, talk with the language arts or English teachers in your school to see what literature they use in their classrooms. Doing so will avoid overlap.

Inspired by Photographs and Videos

Photographs are one way of engaging our students in content connected to social studies. Peruse newspapers or magazines such as *National Geographic* and *Time* for interesting news photographs that could be used to spark student writing. Or, access collections of intriguing images in books such as *National Geographic The Covers: Iconic Photographs, Unforgettable Stories* by Mark Collins Jenkins, *100 Photographs: The Most Influential Images of All Time* by the Editors of *Time* magazine, and *Humans of New York* by Brandon Stanton. Choose your writing prompt based on the content of the photograph, but remember, general prompts can be just as effective: "I notice …," "I think …," or "Before this happened …"

You can also use photographs within the social studies context to represent various points of view. If you and your students are studying topics such as war, immigration, or the funding of public transportation, you could show photographs of various people. Then, invite students to choose one of the individuals from the images and try to write from that person's perspective: "I believe …" or "I think …" When choosing photographs for this purpose, be sure that the images reveal something about the person. We cannot know for certain what the individual would think or feel, but we can make predictions based on what we see in the photograph. This activity challenges our students to move outside their own viewpoints.

To further engage students in the social studies content, it can be effective to use a variety of media. The Heritage Minutes, created by Historica Canada, are effective brief videos to use with students. Resources such as BrainPop and Discovery Education also have excellent videos and resources specifically targeted to our curriculums.

BrainPop has been developed for elementary and junior high school students. Topics of study within the social studies section of BrainPop include ancient civilizations, culture, elections, democracy, world history, women's history, and geography. They also have videos about specific people relevant to our studies, for example, Anne Frank, Martin Luther King Jr., Malala Yousafzai, Barack Obama, and Adolf Hitler. These videos are accessible to students and can help them understand the content material.

Discovery Education is appropriate for students of all ages. Although it is sometimes perceived as more relevant to our science curriculum, there are many topics appropriate for use within social studies as well. What I appreciate about Discovery Education is the aim to address current events, such as trade negotiations or the immigration controversy, and do so in a way appropriate for our students. Although it can be tempting to use the Internet as a general search, we must be extremely cautious about the content that might appear during the search, through advertising or after a video has finished.

Regardless of the source, always watch the videos first to be sure that they are appropriate for your students.

The website Facing History and Ourselves (www.facinghistory.org) is another resource for secondary teachers. It includes a wide variety of resources (such as videos, articles, images, and lessons) on a wide range of topics (such as democracy, race and history, global immigration, and genocide) that teachers can use with their students.

After watching a short video, my students and I engage in a freewrite. This writing can help our students understand and process the information they have heard within the video. We then watch the video again. I invite students to add to or change their freewrite as they are watching the second time. Doing this allows them to clarify their understanding of information and they become incredibly engaged in the video and, therefore, the content. For longer videos, consider freewriting partway through and at the end. If, for example, you are watching a video over two classes, students could freewrite at the beginning of the second class using the prompt "In the video we began watching yesterday ..." This will activate their knowledge from the day before and set the tone for the remainder of the video.

To Facilitate Comparisons

Our curriculums in social studies often involve a comparison of the past to the present, or one culture to another. We attempt to teach this concept to students in many ways: picture books, novels, videos, and field trips to places such as museums, forts, and homesteads. Perhaps you normally ask your students to create a chart or Venn diagram for the sake of comparisons. An alternative is to consider asking students to create the comparisons chart *after* freewriting.

Freewriting often moves the comparisons to a new level as students learn to put themselves in the shoes of someone from a bygone era or another culture and connect with the facts in a new way. When information is in chart form, it tends to remain more factual; when we add freewriting to the mix, the learning tends to become more personal for the students, helping them to grasp the concepts on a deeper level.

Effective Prompts for Making Comparisons

- "In the past …" and "Today …"
- "One hundred years ago …" and "Now …"
- "If I lived in the past …" and "In my life today …"
- "What I like about living in [current year] …" and "What I do not like about living in [current year] …"
- "In our culture …" and "In the [community of study] culture …"
- "In my country …" and "In [country of study] …"
- "What I like about living in [city or country] …" and "What I do not like about living in [city or country] …"

As you can see, the prompts used for comparison are paired. When freewriting with two prompts, you and your students can respond to both in the same day or on two separate days. If you choose to have the class write two freewrites on the same day, it tends to be more effective if students do not realize they will be writing a second time. For example, they might first complete the freewrite "If I lived in the past …" just as they would any other freewrite; then, afterwards, you could invite them to freewrite using "In my life today …"

To further develop our students' skills of prediction, connection making, and critical thinking, we can add a third prompt: "In the future …" Plan to complete the third freewrite on a subsequent day: three freewrites in one day will overwhelm most students. Begin the lesson by asking students to reread their first two freewrites ("If I lived in the past …" and "In my life today …") without explaining why. Then, jump into the prompt "In the future …" After students have written multiple freewrites for the purpose of comparisons, be sure to save time for them to share their observations about the thoughts and realizations generated in their writing.

To Foster Metacognitive Thinking

Writing about an idea *before* you study it and then again *after* you study it yields interesting results. Imagine your students' responses before you delve into the teaching of a concept and then how their thinking and understandings will have changed after your unit. For example, if the focus of study is on government, democracy, rights, and freedoms, there are many possibilities for the use of freewriting:

Prompts such as these can be generated with any topic of study.

Democracy is …	Living in a democracy means …
Freedom is …	It is my right to …

After the unit of study, students enjoy comparing their two freewrites using the same prompt but written weeks apart. Engaging in the process of metacognition tends to build confidence as students recognize how much they have learned.

Cultural Connections

In some form or another, our curriculums deal with culture, citizenship, and identity. With the events taking place in our world today, these topics are particularly relevant: rarely a day goes by without talk in the media about migration and immigration. These topics of study become more interesting to our students when we can connect them to students' own lives. Daniels, Bizar, and Zemelman (2001) speak of this in the high school classroom, but it holds true at any age:

> One simple and powerful way to make social studies or English authentic is to conduct a personal historical investigation, focusing on each student's own family history. Students study their roots, interview their relatives, and learn family stories that they connect and compare to the history of the country. (115)

The idea of giving our students an assignment to research their own ancestry is not new: to talk to their parents, grandparents, and even great grandparents if possible, to determine their country of origin and, if applicable, their immigration journey.

If our goal is understanding and connections, imagine the freewriting that could occur after an investigation into their own family origins with simple prompts such as these:

I am …   I have realized …
I am from …   My family …

Another way to increase the relevance of the topic for students is through a guest speaker: a recent immigrant sharing a personal immigration story with your class. This individual might possibly be a student within your school or the parent of one of your students. It is especially effective to hear from multiple people from the same family to consider how their experiences differ depending on their age and roles: a child's perspective compared to a parent's or grandparent's perspective, for instance.

You may want to put more than one prompt on the board for your students' reference. Students can begin the freewrite with one prompt and then move to another one if they choose.

After listening to the guest speaker, students could write using one of these prompts:

I feel …   I have realized …
I didn't know …   Immigration is …
I'm surprised that …

Each of these experiences — doing family research or listening to a guest speaker — could provide opportunity for two freewrites: one before and then one after the experience. Our students' writing becomes livelier and more impassioned if it begins as a freewrite. Asking students to write an essay or informational paragraph is appropriate, of course, but *beginning* with a freewrite will help our students in generating connections, emotional reactions, and first thoughts without pressure of assessment.

Controversial Issues

Many topics in social studies are controversial and involve complex ethical considerations. In *Being the Change: Lessons and Strategies to Teach Social Comprehension*, Sara Ahmed (2018) discusses the need to give our students the opportunity to talk about difficult issues. We all come to the classroom with our own perspectives and our own stories. We will not always agree. Perhaps nothing emphasized this more than the U.S. presidential election in 2016. Conversations about U.S. politics entered our Canadian classrooms regularly and diverse viewpoints quickly became evident. I can only imagine how this is magnified in the United States.

I do not believe that it is the place of teachers to promote our own ideas; I do agree with Sara Ahmed, however, that we can (and should) facilitate conversations about controversial topics. In addition to discussion, freewriting provides our students with opportunities to explore their own viewpoints, examine alternative perspectives, and form opinions. Students can further develop their thinking.

Let's look at an example. If we are studying population growth in the world, there are many aspects to examine and discuss. Before studying (or even identifying) the topic, students can be given one of these prompts: "People are living longer because …" or "Advances in science are …" When students write using these prompts, they tend to focus on the positive aspects of a longer life and the advances in science. Sometimes, it does not even occur to them that there could be negative impacts. The discussion after the freewrites becomes an excellent introduction to the topic of population growth. Depending on the experience and age of your students, controversial and ethical topics related to population growth may surface, as well: assisted suicide, long-term healthcare facilities, and how we care for our aging population.

During the study of this topic you will address reasons for population growth (increased life expectancies, advancements in science and medical treatment, improved food production, improved public health) and problems associated with population growth (food shortages, overcrowding, limited resources, increased pollution). After these lessons or the unit of study, ask students to do another freewrite about the topic using one of these prompts: "I am worried about …" or "I believe …" Once they have done so, tell them to highlight or underline key phrases or words in their freewrite. This process will likely reveal the specific issue they connected to and feel most passionately about. Even though students use the same prompt when writing about controversial issues, the process of freewriting assists them in clarifying their thinking and forming opinions about the topic. The prewriting for a culminating project of the unit has begun.

The assignment? Students write a paragraph or essay, a poster or advertisement, based on the idea that most resonated with them during this unit of study. Capitalize on their specific interests as they try to formulate and finalize their topics. If possible, give the students choice on the form as well. For example, if a student's freewrite focused on food shortages, he might design an advertisement meant to convince others to adopt sustainable practices and avoid waste. If a student's freewrite focused more on scientific advancement, she might write a short essay outlining both the advantages and disadvantages of such advancement.

> The process explored in this example of population growth could be applied to any controversial topic of study.

Current Events

> "We have the ability to humanize the headlines" (Ahmed 2018, 102).

Our already complex world seems to become more complex every day. Watching the news can be troubling. The issues of violence, gun control, immigration, trade, and the threat of nuclear war can be both confusing and overwhelming for students. Engaging our students in age-appropriate conversation about these topics and providing multiple viewpoints can be helpful as they form their opinions and learn to navigate the world.

Social media are both a blessing and a curse. The blessing? An *ease* with which to stay in contact with family and friends, to connect with people on the other side of the world, and to stay informed. And yet, with the pervasiveness of social media, protecting our students from the realities of the world is difficult. Although I do not believe in shielding them entirely, I do wish we had more control of what they see. Talking about violent events is one thing. Watching them — especially repeatedly as is often the case with news outlets or social media — is not healthy. I know the effect that watching the news has on me: I often feel incredible sadness. I wonder how young minds process current events … When given the opportunity, I have heard students voice fear and confusion in addition to the sadness. But what if they do not have an opportunity to voice these concerns? What if they are processing these events alone? How do they make sense of what they see and hear?

Parents used to have more control of when and how to have conversations with their children about current events. Now, before our children arrive home from school, many of them have already viewed the traumatic event that occurred during the day — on their phone or someone else's. Often, the task then falls on us as teachers to speak to the students about what has occurred. Sometimes, it is difficult to proceed: how much information do we share? how do we help our students comprehend and cope without causing more worry or panic? In each moment, we make a professional judgment based on the information our students seem to know and the questions they ask. As difficult as these conversations are, freewriting is an effective way to help our students process what has occurred: each at their own level of understanding.

Freewriting prompts pertaining to a current event can be used after reading about the event, discussing it, or seeing news clips or even photographs. Because our students are often reacting with emotion and questions, the prompts remain quite simple:

I feel …	I believe …	I've heard …
I think …	I wish …	I'm scared that …

Social Justice Opportunities

In my experience, studying controversial issues or current events often inspires our students to act. For example, in reaction to weather-related events, such as hurricanes or wildfires, or a tragic accident, such as the 2018 Humboldt Broncos bus crash, students express a desire to help. Sometimes they want to fundraise; sometimes they want to collect clothing or food; sometimes they want to write letters; sometimes they are inspired to volunteer.

I encourage my students to take the lead on these social justice projects. Whether they fundraise or send cards and letters to those affected, they seem comforted by reaching out. For example, if students have been studying the water crisis in the world, they may be motivated to fundraise for a well in Africa. Books such as *The Water Princess* by Susan Verde and Georgie Badiel, *The Drop in My Drink: The Story of Water on Our Planet* by Meredith Hooper, and *A Cool Drink of Water* by Barbara Kerley can spark interest in the topic. More research can also follow.

Projects like these are enhanced for students if they reflect and write about the experience:

When we wrote letters to …	When we raised $-- for …
I feel fortunate …	I am proud …
I hope …	

Nurturing Citizenship

We return to the wise words of Confucius at the beginning of the chapter: "Study the past if you would define the future." Beyond that, we consider our overall objectives in social studies: to provide students with opportunities to develop attitudes, skills, and knowledge that will enable them to become engaged, active, informed, and responsible citizens. As outgoing U.S. president Barack Obama put it in his farewell address on January 10, 2017, "It falls to each of us to be those anxious, jealous guardians of our democracy; to embrace the joyous task we've been given to continually try to improve this great nation of ours. Because for all our outward differences, we all share the same proud title: Citizen."

To help nurture our students as engaged, active, informed, and responsible citizens, consider the use of these prompts:

In the world today …
When I think about the future, I …
I wouldn't want to see a repeat of
_____ …
I admire the leadership of …

Laws are important because …
I know I am a member of the global community because …
I am responsible for …

"Our stories are singular, but our destination is shared."
— Barack Obama, 2008 presidential victory speech

The study of social studies has a great impact on our students. It assists them in developing and defining their sense of self and their place in the world. When we engage students in writing as a form of thinking and reflection, they are more likely to see how history, culture, and globalism affect their lives and, ultimately, to understand that they each play a role in the world.

8

Freewriting in Mathematics

"Mathematics is not about numbers, equations, computations, or algorithms: it is about understanding."
— William Paul Thurston

Approaches to mathematics and the math curriculum have changed quite dramatically in my lifetime. When I was a student, math was primarily practice and drill. A few decades ago, there was a swing to inquiry-based learning. Results varied. Debates ensued. The result? *Math Wars*, as it has been dubbed! Regardless of where we stand on this issue, our goal in math is likely the same: student understanding.

Although we associate math with numbers and symbols, it is essential for us to note the role of language within our math classes. After all, we teach math *through* language: both instructional language and academic language specific to math. Furthermore, our students use language to process the information we teach. Many teachers have shown a recognition of the importance of language within their math classrooms by introducing the practices of math talk and Math journals. *Math talk* refers to the dedicated time given to students to articulate their thinking in math. Math journals typically include a representation of ideas through a combination of pictures, numbers, and words. Students might complete an entry in their Math journal while at a classroom centre in guided math. Or, the teacher may require an entry from all students after a given lesson. Regardless of how they are used, math talk and Math journals show the increasing understanding of how we use language to represent and clarify our thinking.

Although writing in math occurs less frequently than in other subject areas, it has its place and seems to be a growing trend.

> In our classroom, we might also choose to include a math word wall which assists students in using mathematical terminology when talking and writing about math.

Constructing Meaning, Clarifying Thinking

We do not ask our students to write in math simply to write: as always, the writing must have purpose. The most important function of writing in mathematics is to help students construct meaning. Math curriculums consistently refer to students *sharing and communicating mathematical understanding*, *reflecting on their work*, and *contextualizing their learning*. Freewriting in math class assists with meeting all these objectives.

Perhaps you have been teaching math for many years and have not found it necessary for students to write during math class. In *So You Have to Teach Math? Sound Advice for Grades 6–8 Teachers*, Cheryl Rectanus (2006) suggests,

Talking and writing helps students make sense of mathematics and think more clearly and deeply about what they are learning. When students write, they have to organize and reflect on their thinking and revisit their ideas. Writing provides an opportunity for students to reinforce and extend their thinking. (83)

Still not convinced? In her book *Math in Plain English: Literacy Strategies for the Mathematics Classroom*, Amy Benjamin (2013, xxii) says this: "Writing causes learning. By writing, we create, transform, mobilize, integrate, and secure what might otherwise be fragile knowledge. Writing whips learning into shape!"

When we watch students complete their work in math, we realize that sometimes they follow the steps and solve the problem and yet do not really understand *what* or *why* they are doing what they are doing. When they write about the experience of solving their math problems, however, they are forced to articulate what they did and why, which helps them monitor their learning and reinforce their understanding. This act of *thinking* through writing, then, often helps students feel more capable and confident about the math itself. If students choose to share their freewriting in math, teachers will also gain insight into student thinking, allowing for more effective feedback and targeted strategies.

Keep in mind that freewriting in math tends to result in less writing than in other subject areas. This is a general tendency, not a reflection on your students.

What do we do with our freewrites in math?

Most of our freewriting in math is a documentation of our students' thinking and, therefore, there is no need to take this writing to a published stage. The only time I may have students create a more finished version of their writing in math is if they are going to share this work with parents or include it as part of a portfolio. Freewriting in math is generally not the time to teach specific writing skills, but since students have an audience for their work, it is a good time to remind them to revise for clarity and edit for readability.

Inspired by Picture Books

Just as in other subject areas, picture books can motivate our students and activate background knowledge. Some of the math concepts within these books are obvious and some, subtle. You can gear prompts specifically to the concepts within a book. For a more general reaction, try these:

There are fewer quality picture book options connected to math as compared to other subject areas. Furthermore, the books with connections to math tend to be geared for younger students.

I relate to this book because …
I noticed …
This book is about math because …
I think we read this book because …

The author used math to …
[Insert character name] used math when …

Picture Books for Use in Mathematics		
Book Title	**Author(s)**	**Topic, Themes**
The Action of Subtraction	Brian P. Cleary	Subtraction
Alexander Who Used to Be Rich Last Sunday	Judith Viorst	Money concepts
Animals by the Numbers: A Book of Infographics	Steve Jenkins	Data, number concepts
The Boy Who Loved Math: The Improbable Life of Paul Erdos	Deborah Heiligman	Biography of a mathematician
Chicken Soup with Rice	Maurice Sendak	Months of the year
The Doorbell Rang	Pat Hutchins	Division
Fraction Fun	David A. Adler	Fractions
A Fraction's Goal — Parts of a Whole	Brian P. Cleary	Fractions
Fractions in Disguise	Edward Einhorn	Fractions
Full House: An Invitation to Fractions	Dayle Ann Dodds	Fractions
The Girl with a Mind for Math: The Story of Raye Montague	Julia Finley Mosca	Biography, Amazing Scientists series
Grandma's Button Box	Linda Williams Aber	Sorting
The Grapes of Math	Greg Tang	Math riddles, counting, patterning
How Big Is it?	Ben Hillman	Size, comparisons
How Much Is a Million?	David M. Schwartz	Number concepts
If You Made a Million	David M. Schwartz	Money concepts, place value
If You Were a Polygon	Marcie Aboff	Geometry
If You Were a Quadrilateral	Molly Blaisdell	Geometry
Infinity and Me	Kate Hosford	Number sense, infinity
The King's Chessboard	David Birch	Exponential growth
Margaret and the Moon: How Margaret Hamilton Saved the First Lunar Landing	Dean Robbins	Biography of Margaret Hamilton; math in the real world
Math Curse	Jon Scieszka	Real-world math connections, math reasoning
Mathemagic! Number Tricks	Lynda Colgan	Number sense
The Mission of Addition	Brian P. Cleary	Addition
Multiplying Menace: The Revenge of Rumpelstiltskin	Pam Calvert	Multiplication
Mystery Math: A First Book of Algebra	David A. Adler	Simple algebra
One Gray Mouse	Katherine Burton	Counting

Picture Books for Use in Mathematics		
Book Title	**Author(s)**	**Topic, Themes**
100th Day Worries	Margery Cuyler	100th day of school
One Hundred Hungry Ants	Elinor J. Pinczes	Division
Out for the Count: A Counting Adventure	Kathryn Cave	Counting to 100
Perfect Square	Michael Hall	Geometry
Perimeter, Area and Volume: A Monster Book of Dimensions	David A. Adler	Perimeter, area, volume
A Remainder of One	Elinor J. Pinczes	Division, remainders
A Second, a Minute, a Week with Days in It	Brian P. Cleary	Units of time
Sir Cumference Math Adventure Series	Cindy Neuschwander	Many topics in this series
Sort It Out	Barbara Mariconda	Sorting, attributes
Spaghetti and Meatballs for All: A Mathematical Story	Marilyn Burns	Area, perimeter
Ten Seeds	Ruth Brown	Subtraction, counting backwards
Two Ways to Count to Ten: A Liberian Folktale	Ruby Dee	Skip counting
Whole-y Cow! Fractions Are Fun	Taryn Souders	Fractions

Inspired by Videos

Resources such as Mathletics, BrainPop, and Discovery Education have excellent videos specifically targeted to math curriculums. Sharing any of them with your class can be followed up by freewriting.

For example, take BrainPop. This resource has been developed for elementary and junior high school students. Topics of study within the mathematics section of BrainPop include algebra, statistics, probability, measurement, geometry, data analysis, ratio, and percentage. These videos are accessible to students, can help them understand the content material, and lead naturally into a freewrite.

If you have access to Discovery Education, you will notice a section titled Virtual Field Trips which enables students to see how math is used in the world every day. Archived field-trip videos include trips to Wall Street, NASA (National Aeronautics and Space Administration), and the headquarters of the National Basketball Association.

Often, a prompt will become obvious to you when you watch the video; otherwise, try a prompt like one of these:

I was surprised that …   I'm excited to …
I didn't know …   I think …
This makes me think of …   This reminds me of …

Watching the videos and the subsequent writing about the videos can help activate background knowledge, uncover misconceptions about a math concept or unit of study, and help students understand how math is used in the real world.

Writing as Reflection

Some teachers ask their students to complete their reflection in the form of a letter to their parents or the teacher, providing an audience. If this is an approach you decide to take, ensure that your students can revise and edit. They should never have to share or hand in a raw freewrite.

Freewriting in math is an excellent reflection tool; the process helps students solidify their understanding and identify confusions or difficulties. When students reflect on math concepts or their math process in writing, their thinking becomes clearer and their confidence tends to improve. After a lesson, students could freewrite using one of these prompts:

Today in math …	I'm confused about …
I knew I was right when …	I noticed …
Next time I would …	I saw a pattern when I …
I am proud of myself for …	I was surprised that …
I still need help with …	

At the Start or the End of a Unit or Term

Writing as reflection is also effective at the beginning and end of a unit or term. When a unit is first introduced through discussion, questions, a book, or even a video, ask your students to freewrite using one of the following prompts:

I predict …	What I know about _____ so far
I expect this unit to be …	is …
I already know …	Algebra [Probability, Geometry]
This math unit reminds me of …	is …

At the end of a *unit*, students can reflect on their learning with one of these prompts:

During this unit in math …	Algebra [Probability, Geometry]
During this unit in math, I	is …
learned …	I improved my understanding of
During this unit in math, I felt …	_____ by …
This math unit reminds me of …	

At the end of a *term*, students can reflect through use of any of these prompts:

During this term in math …	During this term in math, I felt …
During this term in math, I	My goals in math …
learned …	

To Reveal Feelings about Math

"Math is …" is an effective prompt as the year begins and as the year goes on because it allows us to see whether student attitudes or perspectives have changed. Although we give our students the option of sharing their writing in other subject areas, too, I find that students are especially eager to share when this is the prompt.

Some students find math especially challenging so the subject is not always the most popular. Understanding how our students *feel* about math can assist us in determining how best to approach the concepts and better help our students.

Math is …	I find math easy …
I like math because …	I find math difficult …
I dislike math because …	

Sometimes when students articulate their true feelings about math, they feel validated and more willing to take risks. Math may become less intimidating because they have voiced their anxiety about it and perhaps heard others do the same.

Consider using the opposite prompts "I like math because …" and "I dislike math because …" on the same day. Or, put both prompts on the board for students to choose from during the freewrite. Students may choose to use only one or perhaps float between the two. Either option is acceptable, and their choice of prompt will reveal their overriding emotion towards the subject.

To Document Thinking

"I believe writing provides us with another powerful vehicle for helping students become better mathematical thinkers" (Dacey 2018, 9).

When we look at the work our students complete in math, it is sometimes difficult to decipher what they were thinking or what went wrong. Periodically, I have students freewrite on a specific problem they have solved so that their thinking will be made more visible and transparent.

I solved this problem by …	I learned …
I used these steps …	The relationship between …
I know …	My thinking changed …

We can also use freewriting to help our students articulate the specific strategies they are using. For example, when we are teaching basic fact strategies in elementary school, such as *counting on*, *doubles*, *near doubles*, or *skip counting*, and students are practising these strategies, we might ask them to write about their practice:

Today during math games …	I like using the _____ strategy
I used the _____ strategy …	because …

These prompts are effective if used after time engaged in guided math or after students have worked on a math app, for example. The freewriting holds the students more accountable for purposeful practice. Furthermore, if they forgot to utilize the strategies during their practice time, it becomes obvious to them when it is time to write about them!

To Support Inquiry-Based Learning

Sometimes we provide students with more open-ended questions or tasks to solve. During this inquiry-based learning, students are expected to use both prior knowledge and reasoning skills to explore answers to a given question. There is not one right answer or one right approach to these questions; instead, there is a variety of possible answers and approaches. Open-ended questions typically provide natural differentiation, allowing students at different ability levels to engage in the question as they are able.

Perhaps we give students one of these questions:

- Besides 3/4, what fractions are equivalent to the decimal 0.75?
- A number has been rounded to 19.8. What might the number be?
- How are the numbers 90 and 110 alike? different?

As you can see, the questions have many answers. They can also be solved using a number of approaches. I would not give the students instruction on how to solve the question I assign; I would invite them to experiment and explore.

With these prompts, freewriting can be helpful as part of this inquiry process:

Today I discovered …   I noticed …
I wonder why …   I wish I knew more about …
I wonder if …

In their book *Math Is Language Too*, Phyllis Whitin and David J. Whitin (2000) suggest, "When children have regular invitations to write and talk about mathematics in open-ended ways, they soon recognize they can discover new ideas in the process" (3).

If you want students to capture a sequence during the inquiry process, it can be helpful to have the following combination of prompts on the board for them: "First I …," "Next …," "Then …," and "Finally …" Students freewrite as normal but they begin each paragraph with a new prompt.

Math beyond the Classroom

Math surrounds us. Even though students often do not understand when they will use fractions, exponents, or algebra beyond school, freewriting can help them reflect on the relevance of math in their lives. Our brains are constantly looking for and making connections. As Caine and Caine (1991) suggest, "Because the learner is constantly searching for connections on many levels, educators need to orchestrate the experiences from which learners extract understanding" (5). Freewriting is the opportunity to facilitate these connections. The following prompts encourage our students to think beyond math class to the use of math in the wider world:

Math is used …   Last week my mom [dad] used
Last week I used math when I …   math when she [he] …
I use math outside of school when   I remember when …
  I …   A possible career in math …

To facilitate cross-curricular connections, try a prompt like this:

Geologists [politicians, structural engineers, pilots, teachers, veterinarians, nurses] use math when …

With so much content to cover in our curriculum, our students cannot freewrite about everything. Nor should they. When we use writing in math, it is with balance and careful consideration of when it will enhance our students' learning. There is no strict guideline on how often our students should write in math; instead, freewriting in math is to be utilized intentionally. When that happens, it will be a useful tool.

Once students begin to engage in writing during math class, it becomes a natural process and one they come to expect. They become better at explaining their thinking both through talk and writing. Best yet, they become more confident mathematicians!

9

Freewriting in Science

"It's not the answer that enlightens, but the question."
— Eugene Ionesco

Full disclosure: I do not have a scientific brain. I was reminded of this truth as I walked through our local aviation museum. I looked at the airplanes on display — the fuselage, engines, cockpits, and rudders — and I was truly baffled as to how they work. I was even more baffled (and amazed) as to how someone could create them. How does a massive structure such as a 747 become, and stay, airborne? Even after reading the accompanying display signs, I nod and smile, marvel at the creation before me, but really, I do not understand. I respect and admire those who imagine and create technology to advance our world. My brain works differently.

It is for precisely this reason that freewriting is effective for me, and for all those students like me, in science. Freewriting gives our students the opportunity to process ideas and concepts: to think things through and articulate questions. Fortunately, it also assists those students with scientific brains. For them, freewriting is an exciting opportunity where they can demonstrate their understanding and push their thinking further.

When I think back to my own experience as a student in science, the writing I remember most was copying notes. Copious notes. I was not focused on the content while I was writing; I was simply racing to keep up. Yet rarely did I ever read those notes again. They did little to assist me in understanding the content or concepts being taught. I would venture to say that my experience was not unique.

Thankfully, writing in science is now more than notetaking.

If one of our teaching goals is to activate students' thinking skills, then writing can assist us in achieving this. Recall and comparison are necessary and useful skills; however, our students can google anything in seconds. Recalling information is one thing; understanding how it relates to us as individuals and to the whole of society, to the past and to our future, is much more critical.

Curriculum has undergone significant changes to reflect the changes in society. Alberta Education, for example, has outlined eight competencies to reflect our current goals of education: critical thinking, problem solving, managing information, creativity and innovation, communication, collaboration, cultural and global citizenship, and personal growth and well-being. These competencies cross disciplinary boundaries. A document published by Alberta Education in September 2016 states, "Competencies are combinations of knowledge, skills and attitudes that students develop and apply for successful learning, living and working" (1). Freewriting can assist our students in bringing their knowledge, skills, and attitudes together.

Learning to Write like Scientists

Scientific writing tends to be quite technical. As science teachers, we teach our students to write like scientists with a focus on elements such as text features, evidence, observations, content vocabulary, and the sequencing of steps. If students are taking their writing in science to a published level, it is likely in the form of a lab report, an informational text, or a persuasive piece backed by data and evidence. Regardless of which form, "Learning to write like a scientist happens through purposeful instruction that offers scaffolding, practice, and lots of formative feedback" (Grant, Fisher, and Lapp 2015, 95). Students will learn to use concise, scientific language that is information and evidence based. They will analyze information, form an argument, and provide evidence to support their claims. Even if the initial ideas are generated during a freewrite, we can take the time to teach our students how to revise their work so that they are writing like scientists with concise language and evidence backing their claims.

Making Meaning, Finding Relevance

In addition to learning to write like scientists, our students will write to help construct meaning within the science curriculum. The language used within science curriculums supports this process. For example, students will *develop an understanding, construct knowledge*, and *analyze and interpret data*. Students are also asked to predict, observe, infer, question, and classify. Writing about science can help students comprehend vocabulary and understand how things work. It can also help students ask questions and solve problems through their writing.

Because it is often hands-on and elicits our students' curiosity and sense of wonder, science is exciting and engaging to many of our students. In *Reading and Writing in Science*, the authors state, "Science is an integral part of life, and knowing how to think about it, talk about it, and write about it, is empowering" (Grant, Fisher, and Lapp 2015, 16). Freewriting in science helps make the content relevant to students and helps them understand how it affects their everyday world. Science surrounds us.

Freewriting in science (and students sharing their freewriting voluntarily) sometimes reveals misconceptions that students have about the world and how things work. By listening carefully when students share, we note their background knowledge on the topic and the misconceptions they hold, and then later, we can address those misconceptions during the unit of study.

Inspired by Literature

As in other subjects, literature can be used to spark an interest in a topic in science. Fiction books connected to a science topic of study will help to engage students; nonfiction books can become supplementary informational texts. There are books available on most topics of study, especially for our elementary school students, but consider them for the older students as well. You will notice multiple books by the same author on my list below. If you discover a good book by an author, check to see what else that author has published.

When deciding on a prompt in response to literature, we often make it specific to the book we have chosen: for example, "Dinosaurs are ...," "The ocean ...," "Jane Goodall ...," or "An architect ..." General prompts, however, are also effective: "I noticed ...," "I wonder ...," "I learned ...," or even "I think ..." The more often you freewrite, the more naturally you will determine an effective prompt for a given book.

Picture Books for Use in Science		
Book Title	**Author(s)**	**Topic, Themes**
Ada Twist, Scientist	Andrea Beaty	Careers in science
The Animal Book	DK	Animal science
The Barn Owls	Tony Johnston	Life cycles, nature, poetry
Because of an Acorn	Lola M. Schaefer & Adam Schaefer	Ecosystems
A Beetle Is Shy	Dianna Hutts Aston	Insects
The Boy Who Harnessed the Wind	William Kamkwamba & Bryan Mealer	Electricity, invention
Bugs from Head to Tail	Stacey Roderick	Bugs
A Butterfly Is Patient	Dianna Hutts Aston	Butterflies, life cycles
Cloud Dance	Thomas Locker	Clouds

Picture Books for Use in Science		
Book Title	**Author(s)**	**Topic, Themes**
A Cool Drink of Water	Barbara Kerley	Water conservation
The Curious Guide to Things That Aren't	John D. Fixx & James F. Fixx	Riddles and clues about intangible items: one for each letter of the alphabet (e.g., air, breath …)
The Darkest Dark	Chris Hadfield	Sky science
Dreaming Up: A Celebration of Building	Christy Hale	Building, architecture
An Egg Is Quiet	Dianna Hutts Aston	Eggs, animals, life cycles
Endangered	Tim Flach	Endangered species (real photographs)
Engineering in Our Everyday Lives	Reagan Miller	Engineering
Engineering the ABC's: How Engineers Shape Our World	Patty O'Brien Novak	Engineering
Good Trick, Walking Stick!	Sheri Mabry Bestor	Insects
The Handiest Things in the World	Andrew Clements	Inventions
Have You Seen Bugs?	Joanne Oppenheim	Insects
How Things Work: Discover Secrets and Science behind Bounce Houses, Hovercraft, Robotics, and Everything in Between	T. J. Resler	Physics
Hurricane	David Wiesner	Hurricanes
Iggy Peck, Architect	Andrea Beaty	Careers in science
I Wonder Why the Sea Is Salty and Other Questions about the Oceans	Anita Ganeri	Ocean life
I Wonder Why Stars Twinkle	Carole Stott	Sky science
Knowledge Encyclopedia	DK	General science
The Lorax	Dr. Seuss	Conservation
Many Moons	Rémi Courgeon	Phases of the moon
Me … Jane	Patrick McDonnell	Simple biography of Jane Goodall
Motion, Magnets and More	Adrienne Mason	Physics
Move It! Motion, Forces and You	Adrienne Mason	Physics
My Five Senses	Aliki	The five senses
National Geographic Kids Why? Over 1,111 Answers to Everything	Crispin Boyer	General science
National Geographic Little Kids: The First Big Book of Animals	Catherine D. Hughes	Animal science

National Geographic Little Kids: The First Big Book of Space	Catherine D. Hughes	Sky science
National Geographic Little Kids: The First Big Book of Why	Amy Shields	General science
Natural History (Smithsonian)	DK	Biology
Newton and Me	Lynne Mayer	Physics, laws of motion
Ocean: The Definitive Visual Guide	DK	Oceanography, marine life
Planting the Trees of Kenya	Claire A. Nivola	Importance of trees, using the land wisely, African cultures
A Rock Can Be	Laura Purdie Salas	Rocks and minerals
A Rock Is Lively	Dianna Hutts Aston	Rocks and minerals
Rosie Revere, Engineer	Andrea Beaty	Careers in science
Science Verse	Jon Scieszka	General science (in verse!)
A Seed Is Sleepy	Dianna Hutts Aston	Seeds, flowers and plants
Sky Tree: Seeing Science through Art	Thomas Locker, with Candace Christiansen	Seasonal changes, trees and forests
Stars: A Family Guide to the Night Sky	Adam Ford	Sky science
Water Can Be …	Laura Purdie Salas	Water in our world
Water Dance	Thomas Locker	The water cycle
Water Is Water	Miranda Paul	The water cycle
We Planted a Tree	Diane Muldrow	Importance of trees
Whale in a Fishbowl	Troy Howell	Animals in captivity
What's the Big Idea? Amazing Science Questions for the Curious Kid	Vicki Cobb	General science
Whose Nest Is This?	Heidi Roemer	Nature, birds
Winter Is Coming	Tony Johnston	Seasonal changes, nature
You Can Be a Nature Detective	Peggy Kochanoff	Wonders in nature
Zoobots: Wild Robots Inspired by Real Animals	Helaine Becker	Robotics

Both DK and National Geographic publish many series of books that are appropriate for classroom use. There are different series for a variety of age levels. Even one page of any of these books could be shared to spark our students' thinking and writing.

Novels/Biographies for Use in Science		
Book Title	**Author(s)**	**Topic, Themes**
The Boy Who Harnessed the Wind: Creating Currents of Electricity and Hope	William Kamkwamba & Bryan Mealer	Biography, electricity, invention
Chasing Space (Young Readers' Edition)	Leland D. Melvin	Memoir by NASA astronaut
The Doctor with an Eye for Eyes: The Story of Dr. Patricia Bath	Julia Finley Mosca	Amazing Scientists series
Electrical Wizard: How Nikola Tesla Lit Up the World	Elisabeth Rusch	Biography, electrical engineering, invention
Elon Musk & the Quest for a Fantastic Future (Young Readers' Edition)	Ashlee Vance	Biography, innovation, invention, technology
The Fourteenth Goldfish	Jennifer L. Holm	Eternal youth, immortality
The Girl Who Thought in Pictures: The Story of Dr. Temple Grandin	Julia Finley Mosca	Amazing Scientists series
Grace Hopper: Queen of Computer Code	Laurie Wallmark	Biography, computer coding
Hidden Figures	Margot Lee Shetterly	Biography
Hoot	Carl Hiaasen	Endangered species
On a Beam of Light: The Story of Albert Einstein	Jennifer Berne	Biography
One Plastic Bag: Isatou Ceesay and the Recycling Women of the Gambia	Miranda Paul	Biography, recycling, care for the environment
Star Stuff: Carl Sagan and the Mysteries of the Cosmos	Stephanie Roth Sisson	Astronomy, Carl Sagan
Steve Jobs: Insanely Great	Jessie Hartland	Graphic biography, computers, technology
Steve Jobs: The Man Who Thought Differently	Karen Blumenthal	Biography, computers, technology
The Tree Lady: The True Story of How One Tree-Loving Woman Changed a City Forever	H. Joseph Hopkins	Biography, trees and forests
Women in Science: 50 Fearless Pioneers Who Changed the World	Rachel Ignotofsky	Biography
Whoosh! Lonnie Johnson's Super-Soaking Stream of Inventions	Chris Barton	Biography, invention
A Wrinkle in Time	Madeleine L'Engle	Time travel, invention

Inspired by Photographs, Videos, and Podcasts

As in social studies, it can be effective to use a variety of media to engage our students in the curricular content in science.

Photographs of the natural world can be both breathtaking and thought provoking. Images ranging from those of microscopic creatures to the expanse of the solar system can be used to trigger student writing about science. *National Geographic Stunning Photographs*, with text by Annie Griffiths, and *National Geographic Spectacle: Rare and Astonishing Photographs*, with text by Susan Tyler Hitchcock, are wonderful sources for these images.

Not long ago, I stumbled upon an episode of *The Nature of Things* titled "The Wild Canadian Year" on CBC Television. This episode focused on spring but there is an episode for each season. As I watched, I couldn't help but think how engaging these programs, or snippets of them, would be for our students. The videography is incredible, giving a glimpse into the natural world.

Resources such as Discovery Education and BrainPop also have excellent videos specifically targeted to our science curriculum. Discovery Education is appropriate for students of all ages. BrainPop has been developed for elementary and junior high school students. Topics of study within the science section of BrainPop include photosynthesis, climate change, clouds, chemistry, hibernation, flight, levers, magnets, and constellations. BrainPop also has videos about specific people relevant to our science curriculum: these include Galileo, Charles Darwin, Isaac Newton, Jane Goodall, and Nikola Tesla. These videos are accessible to students and can help them understand content material.

An increasing number of sites create regular podcasts related to content curriculum or based on student questions. These podcasts can be used to spark student interest and provoke writing and discussion. At the time of publishing, these sites were appropriate options for science-related topics:

www.brainson.org	www.howstuffworks.com
www.sciencepodcastforkids.com	www.nationalgeographic.org/topics/ wild-chronicles

Always preview the videos and podcasts to be sure that they are appropriate and a good fit for your students. Some are geared for elementary students, some for high school students, and some for students in between.

As with literature, many of our freewriting prompts for photographs, videos, or podcasts will be specific to the content. Once again, though, general prompts are also effective:

Science is …	I heard …
In science …	[Insert name of scientist or
In nature …	inventor] is [was] …
I noticed …	[Insert topic of study] is …
I think …	

Experiments

Many of our science outcomes involve the exploration of concepts through experiments. Freewriting fits wonderfully into this process because it helps students in making predictions and observations, and in learning how to sequence.

Even when using a visual prompt, remember to give your students a word prompt as well. Doing this will ensure that they can keep writing by rewriting the prompt as necessary.

Podcasts also provide our students with the opportunity to be critical consumers of information.

Prediction

Once you have set up an experiment and discussed what you are going to do, students could do a short freewrite to the prompt "I predict …" It is essential to remind our students, especially our young students, that predictions do not have to be correct; however, we can teach them to use their background knowledge and powers of observation to make their best guesses.

Observation

It is effective to ask our students to write about what they saw during an experiment. Even before they complete a lab report, they could freewrite about their observations. Taking this step will assist them in understanding what has occurred, why it has occurred, and why it is important.

I observed …	I think …
I noticed …	I think this happened because …
I think this means …	This is important because …
I'm confused about …	

Sequencing

The use of experiments can assist our students with the skill of sequencing. In science it becomes obvious to students that completing steps in a set order is important. After they have written about their observations, we could ask them to look for words such as *first, second, next, finally*. If they haven't used transition words such as these, they could add them in, where appropriate. We can also teach our students the importance of writing the various steps clearly and accurately to ensure validity.

In their writing about experiments, students can also check to see whether they have used content vocabulary, highlighting or underlining any key words they find. If they haven't used specific content vocabulary, they can add it to the writing after the fact. This activity not only improves the writing they are working on, but also tends to help them use more specific language in future writing.

Wonderings and Inquiry

The premise of the science curriculum is to inspire a sense of wonder in the world around us. The content knowledge within the science curriculum is specific to each grade level, but the skills within the curriculum are similar: prediction, inquiry, inferencing, experimentation, investigation, observation, creation, and problem solving.

After Stephen Hawking died, I heard a recording of him speaking these words: "So remember to look up at the stars and not down at your feet. Try to make sense of what you see and wonder about what makes the universe exist. Be curious." To help encourage this sense of wonder and curiosity in our students, we can invite them to freewrite about a topic before beginning the unit of study. It doesn't matter if you will be studying insects, plant life, wetland ecosystems, rocks and minerals, volcanoes, space, cellular biology, chemical reactions, or momentum. The following prompts can activate our students' background knowledge and provide the beginnings for student inquiry:

Insert the name of the topic you are studying.

I wonder if …   I'm curious about …

I wonder why …   Insects …

Adding the word *if* to our prompts can also effectively elicit student wonderings. These prompts could be connected to a unit of study or stand alone. Consider these examples:

If I were a scientist, I would study …   If I could invent anything, I would invent …

If cars had never been invented …   If dinosaurs were still alive …

If there was a water shortage in the world …   If there were no spiders on Earth …

If I could travel through space …   If I lost the sense of sight …

If I could cure …   If there was no gravity …

These prompts can be used to activate prior knowledge, stimulate interest in a topic, or become an exercise in brainstorming. I use these prompts once students have had some practice freewriting. Even still, be aware that these types of prompts sometimes cause the writing to flow more slowly than during a typical freewrite: students are *thinking*. Students may need reminders to write the first thing they think of and not censor themselves when writing. Again, be sure to allow students to share *all*, *some*, or *none* of the writing.

Another strategy to foster a sense of curiosity about the world is to create a heart map of wonderings. Heard (2016) includes a template called "What I Wonder about Heart Map" in her book *Heart Maps: Helping Students Create and Craft Authentic Writing*. I recommend that students begin it on one day and add to it throughout the year as they think of more questions and thoughts.

All of these prompts and the freewriting that flows from them can be used to inspire student research and inquiry projects.

The Potential of Makerspaces

Over the last few years, we have seen the maker movement flourish. More and more schools and public libraries have a Makerspace within. These spaces provide students with hands-on learning opportunities to explore, learn, build, and create, often in open-ended, student-driven ways. As teachers, we play quite different roles in a Makerspace than we do traditionally. Instead of teaching explicitly, we are facilitating our students' learning.

As teachers we are still finding our way with these spaces. In some situations, I have noticed that students are not always held accountable for their time or given time to reflect on what worked and what didn't. To me, what makes these spaces especially powerful is the opportunity they provide for metacognition and higher-level thinking.

Students are quite naturally engaged in a Makerspace setting. Students who seem to get the most out of the experience, however, are those who can reflect and talk about their learning. To help facilitate this reflection and thinking, and to hold them accountable for their time, students complete a short freewrite at the end of the session using simple prompts such as "Today I discovered …," "Today I created …," or "I was surprised that …" Talk about constructing meaning! If we learn by *doing*, we learn even more by *writing about our doing* afterwards. Interacting with students throughout the process with comments such as

"Tell me what you are working on" or "What have you discovered today?" can also help students when it comes time to write about their day in Makerspace.

By building this writing time into the routine of Makerspace, students will have a record of their thinking and learning regardless of whether they are coding; using robotics, Lego, Minecraft, pottery, wheels and levers, a 3-D printer, drones, or textiles; or woodworking. This writing time can also lead to powerful sharing time as students learn from each other's processes and become excited about and interested in experimenting with different materials. After all, that's what Makerspace is all about: the process, not necessarily a product.

The Addition of Drawings to Freewriting in Science

In science we attempt to stimulate our students' observation skills. Whether it be during an experiment, inquiry-based learning, or experiences in nature, science concepts lend themselves to drawing and labeling. Consider adding this as an additional step to the freewriting process in science. The writing time remains writing time, but drawing and labeling could easily be added either before or after it.

Writing and Drawing in a Designated Notebook

Generally, I suggest that teachers use loose-leaf paper for student freewriting regardless of the subject area; however, freewriting in Makerspace is one exception to this. It is useful to create a Makerspace Notebook or a Maker Notebook. Students can keep a record of their thoughts all together and include drawings, photographs, and such if they wish. The freewriting completed during Makerspace time would rarely be writing that we take to a published state. Just like Makerspace, it is the process that is important, not the product. Every so often, encourage your students to look back and reread their Makerspace freewriting. They typically do so eagerly and excitedly.

I have had some students ask if they can write *before* they begin the day's Makerspace time. Of course! These students wanted to describe their plans in writing. For students writing *before* making, suggest these prompts: "Today I want to try ..." or "I'm thinking ..." I have also watched some students stop what they are doing in Makerspace to write — they wanted to capture the discovery they just made. I provide students with Post-it notes during their Makerspace time to allow them to jot notes as they are working. They then expand on those ideas later during their freewriting time at the end of the Makerspace session.

Some teachers have shared with me that they do not want to ruin the pleasure of Makerspace by asking their students to write. By your building this writing time into your Makerspace schedule, though, *and explaining why* you value it, students will come to understand how the process of documentation can assist them as learners. Keep in mind, too, that the writing time is short compared to the time spent making.

Informational Texts

As mentioned earlier, we sometimes engage our students in writing during science class through the creation of informational text. For elementary students, this might take the form of a poster, a pamphlet, or a short book; for older students, an essay. Regardless, such text often highlights some of the specific features of scientific writing — text features, content vocabulary, and labels among them.

Before students write these informational texts, they can freewrite about the topic. Freewriting in this context becomes brainstorming. When students are finished the freewrite, they can highlight key words, main ideas, topics, or thoughts that they want to incorporate into their text before beginning their research. Freewriting for this purpose may seem an extra step, but students find it useful in generating information and getting started.

Because the freewriting in this situation is intended as brainstorming, prompts are specific and connected closely to the content: "Magnets ...," "Arachnids ...," "Deciduous trees ..."

Ethical Questions

Science, by the nature of the content, inherently presents many ethical considerations: societal, economic, and environmental. In fact, there are ethical questions connected to most areas of the science curriculum. The simplest of questions can be used for our young students. The more complex questions are reserved for older students. For example, students could discuss questions and dilemmas such as these:

- Should families be forced to recycle?
- Should governments place limits on water use?
- How does the release of new versions of cellphones or computers affect the environment?
- How can we sustain our resources for our children, grandchildren, and great grandchildren?
- Should climate change affect our day-to-day decisions?
- Should our governments spend millions or billions of dollars on space exploration or should that money be used for other things?
- Should our society pursue the idea of cloning animals? cloning people?
- Should our city allow driverless cars?
- Should drones be used for parcel delivery?
- Is there a danger of artificial intelligence taking over the world?

In this situation, you and your students will write *after* engaging in a class discussion. If we ask them to write without prior discussion, some of our students might not have enough background knowledge or experience with the topic to write for any length of time. Be sure to write the question on the board as the title students will record, for example, "Should all families be forced to recycle?" Then, provide students with a prompt that applies to the question: "I think ...," "I worry about ...," or "I feel ..." Even though there is no mention of the topic in the prompt, the question on the board (acting as their title) and the discussion that occurs before the writing time will influence the writing.

If you want students to write a piece to publish, you could teach them to take the ideas formulated in the discussion and the subsequent freewriting and then move to a more structured writing assignment where they would review multiple sources, analyze data, and write well-supported arguments.

Writing in Nature

Whether our students are 6 or 16, we can take them into nature and write. If studying plant growth, trees and forests, rocks and minerals, or a type of ecosystem, for example, students can write about them in nature. If you have recently taught a lesson about specific types of trees and details such as their bark, leaves, and seeds, students will likely be drawn to these details. If you have been talking about seasonal changes and you take them out in the spring, they will notice details related to the changes taking place.

When we take our students out of the classroom and into nature, we can inspire them to write, help hone their observation skills, and teach specific concepts. There are many effective prompts in nature. Some are designed to encourage observations and others, a connection to nature. Choose the prompt that applies to your situation and your purpose in the day's writing:

I see …	In nature …
I notice …	My favorite part about being in
I hear …	nature is …
I smell …	I like being outside because …
I feel …	I do not like being outside because
Using my senses, I notice …	…

When they write in nature, students often enjoy adding drawings. Encourage them to sketch what they see either before or after their writing time. Depending on where you are located and the environment around you, you could ask students to draw a specific tree, the leaves, or the larger environment. Encourage them to label their drawings since this practice is common in science.

Children have a natural curiosity about the world around them: why things are the way they are, how things work, and why things happen. As astronomer Carl Sagan has said, "Somewhere, something incredible is waiting to be known." Science leads our students on a journey of discovery; freewriting supports the process and solidifies their learning.

Even if the weather does not lend itself to writing outside, taking a walk outside before writing is motivating for our student writers. Shortly before writing this chapter, for example, I went for a long walk in a rural setting: a blanket of snow covered the trees and land around me, a light breeze filled the air with snowflakes, and the sun shone through the trees, making the snow shimmer and glisten. I felt inspired to write.

10

Freewriting about the Fine Arts

"Without art, the crudeness of reality would make the world unbearable."
— George Bernard Shaw

I am moved by Art. It liberates me. It enlightens me. It motivates and provokes me. It is something I know I need in my life. When my family and I travel, we visit local galleries and we have season's tickets to our city's theatre. After an experience with Art, I often have an intense desire to write. And frequently, this writing is especially powerful. Creativity is triggered by creativity.

I once saw a dramatic, musical performance titled *Old Stock: A Refugee Love Story*. While I was watching, I found myself overcome with emotion. I laughed. I cried. I learned. I considered the circumstances that others have faced. I made connections to my own experience. I left enlightened, inspired, and thoughtful. I left with a desire to write. Through Art, serious topics can be explored, and content, made accessible and relatable. Whether it be visual art such as painting, sculpture, or film, or performance art such as music or theatre, Art can help us to see and understand things in new ways.

As they are not considered core curriculum, the fine arts sometimes find themselves on the chopping block in the world of education. And yet, the fine arts provide a wonderful opportunity to engage our students and enhance their social, emotional, and intellectual well-being. Through the fine arts, students can learn about themselves and the world around them. Through the fine arts, students can cope with the harsh realities they may sometimes face. Our students will not all grow up to be professional musicians, artists, or actors, and we do not expect them to — not all of them are naturally artistic. But, if approached appropriately, Art can be a powerful *experience* for our students regardless of any finished products they create. It is critical to differentiate between product and process. Rubin (2005) explains the potential of Art with children:

> Making art available to more children in a way that allows them to honestly express themselves is good medicine, like taking vitamins or getting regular checkups — a form of primary prevention. (311)

I wholeheartedly believe this to be true. I have witnessed the power of art with a class as a whole and I have witnessed its power with children who have experienced trauma and loss. Should the fine arts go on the chopping block in my region, I will be among the first to fight for them.

The fine arts can include programs such as music, the visual arts, dance, and drama. This chapter will focus on music and the visual arts although the suggestions can be adapted for dance and drama, as well.

For many, teaching the fine arts can be a challenge. Some teachers are specialists in these areas: their musical or artistic talents strong. Other teachers find themselves teaching the fine arts without a lot of education or expertise in the field. Regardless of your education or experience in this area, I expect freewriting will be a delightful addition to your program.

Constructing Meaning

Not long ago, I was on a panel interviewing prospective administrators for our school district. After the interviewee left the room, each of us on the panel scored the interview on our own before discussing our impressions with one another. This scoring enabled us to formulate our own thoughts and opinions without being influenced by the others in the room.

I apply the same premise to writing about the fine arts. By inviting them to write about music and visual art, we provide our students with the opportunity to reflect, connect, and form their own opinions about what they hear and see without being influenced by their peers. This opportunity is especially valuable because Art is so subjective. We provide students with a means of turning inward and connecting to the world. We provide them with an opportunity to explore their own thoughts and emotions.

The curriculums for music and the visual arts generally involve two components: an appreciation of the form and the creation of the genre. The writing we do in the fine arts enhances our students' experiences of both appreciating and creating art.

What do we do with our freewrites in the fine arts?

Freewriting in the fine arts is primarily about process and rarely about taking our work through the writing process. Because music and visual art tend to tap into our emotions, the writing we do in these subjects often becomes quite poignant; the sharing time after our freewriting in these areas, therefore, is especially powerful. Thoughts about process, imagination, creativity, and emotional reactions often surface and can lead to interesting discussions. Since these areas are quite subjective, it is important that students are taught to respect the wide range of opinions that may emerge.

We spend little time teaching students to write in the fine arts. If we ask our students to do a written assignment in this area, it is likely a biography of a composer, a comparison of artworks, or an exploration of a theme. A freewrite or two might become the basis for the assignment. If so, students would revise and edit the writing as discussed in Chapter 5.

Inspired by Picture Books

Picture books that incorporate the fine arts are among my favorites. Some expose our students to a particular style. Some introduce a prominent figure in the field. Some discuss the purpose of the arts or the role of the artist in our world. Some simply help us to appreciate the form. A list of recommended titles appears on the next two pages.

Picture Books for Use in the Fine Arts			
Book Title	Author(s)	Illustrator(s)	Topic, Themes
Art	Patrick McDonnell	Patrick McDonnell	Art, composition, line
Art & Max	David Wiesner	David Wiesner	Art, expression
Beautiful Oops!	Barney Saltzberg	Barney Saltzberg	Creativity, imagination
Can You Hear It? (includes CD)	William Lach	Illustrated with works from the Metropolitan Museum of Art	Art and music appreciation
The Dot	Peter H. Reynolds	Peter H. Reynolds	Creativity, individuality
Drum City	Thea Guidone	Vanessa Brantley-Newton	Creating music
Drum Dream Girl: How One Girl's Courage Changed Music	Margarita Engle	Rafael López	Music
Firebird	Misty Copeland	Christopher Myers	Dance
Frederick	Leo Lionni	Leo Lionni	Purpose of art/artists in our world
Imagine a Day	Sarah L. Thomson	Rob Gonsalves	Imagination, creativity
Imagine a Night	Sarah L. Thomson	Rob Gonsalves	Imagination, creativity
Ish	Peter H. Reynolds	Peter H. Reynolds	Expression, creativity
John's Secret Dreams: The Life of John Lennon	Doreen Rappaport	Bryan Collier	Music (John Lennon)
Josephine: The Dazzling Life of Josephine Baker	Patricia Hruby Powell	Christian Robinson	Dance, civil rights
Little Melba and Her Big Trombone	Katheryn Russell-Brown	Frank Morrison	Biography (Melba Liston), jazz
The Man with the Violin	Kathy Stinson	Dušan Petričić	Music appreciation
M is for Melody: A Music Alphabet	Kathy-Jo Wargin	Kathy-Jo Wargin	Music appreciation
Mix It Up!	Hervé Tullet	Hervé Tullet	Color mixing
The Most Magnificent Thing	Ashley Spires	Ashley Spires	Creativity, invention
The Museum	Susan Verde	Peter H. Reynolds	Art appreciation
Musical Instruments Believe	Dorothy K. Ederer, Christopher W. Tremblay, Dan Friedt, and Joanne Friedt	Donna Mitchell-Collins	Musical instruments, expression
Music: The Definitive Visual History	DK		Music history
Playing from the Heart	Peter H. Reynolds	Peter H. Reynolds	Music, performance art

Picture Books for Use in the Fine Arts			
Book Title	**Author(s)**	**Illustrator(s)**	**Topic, Themes**
Robert Batemen: The Boy Who Painted Nature	Margriet Ruurs	Robert Bateman	Painting
Rock and Roll Highway	Sebastian Robertson	Adam Gustavson	Music (Robbie Robertson)
Satchmo's Blues	Alan Schroeder	Floyd Cooper	Music (Louis Armstrong)
Seen Art?	Jon Scieszka	Lane Smith (also includes artwork of many famous artists)	Art appreciation
Sky Color	Peter H. Reynolds	Peter H. Reynolds	Creativity, inspiration
Wait! No Paint!	Bruce Whatley	Bruce Whatley	Art crossing boundaries
When the Beat Was Born: DJ Cool Herc and the Creation of Hip Hop	Laban Carrick Hill	Theodore Taylor III	Biography (Clive Campbell), hip hop music
The Whisper	Pamela Zagarenski	Pamela Zagarenski	Storytelling, imagination
Why Is Blue Dog Blue?	George Rodrigue	George Rodrigue	Art, color, imagination
You Can't Take a Balloon into the Metropolitan Museum	Jacqueline Preiss Weitzman	Robin Glasser	Relationships between art and life
Zin! Zin! Zin! A Violin	Lloyd Moss	Marjorie Priceman	Music appreciation, instrument identification

When you read a book from the list to your students, a prompt will likely become obvious. Some general prompts that are effective include these:

This book …
In this book …
I liked the way …
Art is …

Music is …
I am creative when …
Imagine the world without …
The pictures …

The books on the list above are *about* the fine arts; however, I use picture books for inspiration for many of my art lessons because of their beautiful illustrations, regardless of the topic of the book. For example, the book *Happy* by Mies van Hout has colorfully illustrated fish on each page, each with a different emotion. Although the *topic* of this book is not art, the artwork itself inspires the lesson. A quick visit to your bookshelf will likely yield many books that can inspire art lessons in this way.

Inspired by Video

BrainPop has extensive, appropriate topics for the fine arts. A few examples:

- Art: cubism, impressionism, surrealism, pop art, portraits, sculpture, animation …
- Music: brass instruments, string instruments, percussion and woodwinds, scales, clefs and time signatures, melody and harmony …

- Famous artists and musicians: Georgia O'Keeffe, Leonardo da Vinci, Ludwig van Beethoven, Louis Armstrong, Wolfgang Amadeus Mozart …

These videos are accessible to students and can help them understand our content material. After seeing a video, students could write in response to prompts like these:

My first impression of _____ is …	I'm surprised that …
_____ is …	I'd like to know more about …

For older students, consider the option of TED Talks to provoke thought or divergent thinking. One of my favorites on the topic of Art is *Tidying Up Art* by Ursus Wehrli. After watching this video, students could respond to the prompt "In this TED Talk …," "Ursus Wehrli tidied up Art by …," or "Ursus Wehrli made me laugh because …" Other possible TED Talks to inspire writing include *How Yarn Bombing Grew into a Worldwide Movement* (Magda Sayeg) and *Art Made of Storms* (Nathalie Miebach). Be sure to preview the entire TED Talk before using it with your students to determine the appropriateness of the content for your context: TED Talks are not designed for children.

Music Experiences

Some of the objectives within the music curriculum include an enjoyment of music, an appreciation and awareness of a variety of types of music, an awareness of instruments, self-expression through music, and an understanding of various musical skills. Freewriting can easily be used to enhance the music program regardless of the grade level you teach. As I noted in the introduction to this book, I have had music teachers attend my sessions on freewriting: they have been pleasantly surprised to see how this process applies to their teaching.

Writing while Listening to Music

Writing while listening to music is a powerful experience. Music conveys such a variety of moods and emotions. When we write to music, different parts of our brain are stimulated. Be sure to try writing to music in a range of genres for the full experience.

The writing we do at this time could flow from one of the general prompts discussed in Chapter 3, such as "In my family …," "I am …," or "Friendship is …" However, we could also offer prompts directly related to the music experience. Because people experience music in very personal ways, I tend to put two prompts on the board to ensure that all students can respond successfully. Here are some prompts I commonly use:

Music is …	Music is like poetry because …
This music …	My favorite song is …
This music makes me feel …	Singing is …
This music reminds me of …	In my house …
I like music because …	

Although "In my house …" does not seem to directly relate, while listening to music, students often write about the role, if any, that music plays in their home.

It can be powerful to expose our students to professional musicians either by bringing in guests to the school or taking students on a field trip. Many students do not have the opportunity to listen to a soloist, quartet, symphony, or opera, if not with the school. Many orchestras and symphonies have programs created specifically for students.

Writing after Creating Music

Students create music in music class: sometimes individually but most often in harmony with others. They sing, use percussion instruments, and play woodwind instruments; our older students might be exposed to string and brass instruments, as well. The experience of creating music causes joy in some students and trepidation or downright fear in others. To explore the emotions connected to the experience, students could respond to a prompt like one of these:

When I make music, I feel …	Making music is …
I like to play …	Harmony is …
When I play …	My favorite instrument …

Cultural Connections

Music is created in every part of the world and closely tied to tradition and culture, each with its own unique style and sound, rhythm and expression. Regardless of whether students are Indigenous, new to the country, or, like me, third-generation citizens, invite them to research music from their own culture or family background and, if possible, bring music to share. If you are fortunate, sometimes this request leads to a visit from a family member who plays an instrument (though this is not the expectation). When we listen to the sounds from around the world, we can reference a map (even making short notes about what we hear) and then listen for similarities and differences between the music of various regions. Depending on what we want them to focus on, our students could learn to recognize the sounds of various instruments; the nature of music — lyrical or instrumental; the style of music; or the mood created. Try one of the following prompts to help students reflect on the music of various cultures:

Music from my culture makes me feel …	I like the music from …
	Music from around the world …
Music from my culture reminds me of …	I noticed …

Music in Our World

Give your students this simple homework assignment: *Over the next week, listen for music in our world. Keep a list of where you hear it.*

Students may be surprised at all the places they hear music without usually giving it much thought: elevators, stores, movies, television shows, the ice-cream truck, as well as more obvious places such as the radio. After the week is up, work together to create a long class list of places where your students heard music. Then, freewrite about music in our world using one or two of these prompts:

Music is used to …	I noticed music …
I was surprised to hear music …	If we didn't have music …

Student Picks

The music we teach and play for our students is likely different than what they would listen to on their own time. Consider assigning one student per week to share a favorite song or piece of music. Create a sign-up sheet for students to choose when they would like to share. Some might have a piece of music in mind immediately when we give this assignment; others might need time to think about and search for something to share. Students are responsible for informing you of their choice ahead of time, bringing the music to class and, of course, ensuring that it is appropriate for the school environment.

This time spent sharing each week is short but goes a long way to build positive relationships with our students. They will feel valued and appreciated for who they are and the style of music they enjoy.

Every so often students could freewrite about the Student Picks:

I've noticed …	My favorite Student Pick was …
I connected to the music _____ brought because …	I like the line …
	My favorite music …

Visual Art Experiences

When we teach art to students, sometimes the emphasis is on creating artwork. And yet, the curriculum involves so much more. An examination of art curriculums at various levels reveals that all include an aspect of appreciation. In Alberta, the elementary art curriculum focuses on four components of visual learning: reflection, depiction, composition, and expression. Within reflection, students study, analyze, compare, and connect with art. Although they can do this orally to some extent, using the process of freewriting will enable all students to become engaged in the reflection, not only those with the most eager hands in the air. Freewriting allows our students to consider what artists might be expressing through their work, think critically about art in our world and as a reflection of society, make personal connections, and, ultimately, express their insights. Prompts are simple and often ones we have used before. The difference? We have something to look at, something to watch, something we have experienced visually.

Writing while Viewing Art

When choosing a visual prompt to inspire your students, consider their age level and interests. Look for artwork that will elicit some sort of reaction; it may stir emotion, provoke thought, generate story, or create mood. Some of my favorite paintings to use for this purpose include these:

The Nut Gatherers by William-Adolphe Bouguereau
Starry Night by Vincent van Gogh
Habitant Farm by Arthur Lismer
The Jack Pine by Tom Thomson
The Tree of Life, Stoclet Frieze by Gustav Klimt
Good and Bad by George Rodrigue
Ball Game by Ted Harrison
Floating Gulls by Ted Harrison

Runaway by Norman Rockwell
Pop Shop (See No Evil, Hear No Evil, Speak No Evil) by Keith Haring
The Dance of Youth by Pablo Picasso
I Wanna Go by Ron Burns
Shake No. 3 by Rebecca Kinkead
Marshmallow (Twilight) by Rebecca Kinkead
Spring by Giuseppe Arcimboldo
Wanderer above the Sea of Fog by Caspar David Friedrich
The Dance Class by Edgar Degas
The Child's Bath by Mary Cassatt
Sunset Frolic by Theresa Paden

I visited the Moco Museum in Amsterdam and was lucky enough to see exhibits of the street artists Banksy and Icy and Sot. Their work is provocative and challenges us to rethink preconceived notions we might hold. Even the stories of these artists would make for interesting discussions with our older students. Images that would be especially effective with students: *Girl with Balloon* and *Flower Thrower* by Banksy, *Let Her Be Free*, *Shadow*, and *Color Rain* by Icy and Sot.

I keep a collection on a Pinterest board for easy reference. Choose your own favorites and start your own collection.

Even though they have a visual prompt, be sure to give your students a word prompt to keep them writing:

I see …
I notice …
I feel …
I think …

The artist …
I think the artist was feeling …
I'm not sure about …

We can also show our students several pieces of art by one artist and then have them freewrite on the collection of artworks. Sometimes we gain further insight when we look at a group of an artist's paintings. Often, curators plan for this experience when we visit a gallery. Some connections are obvious and some are not. Some are similar in content and some in style. Some use similar techniques and other are quite diverse. When looking at Renoir paintings, students might notice that many include someone reading a book. The art of Degas, both painting and sculpture, often features ballet. When looking at paintings by Van Gogh, students might recognize the similar style and texture created by his thick brush strokes and the illusion of movement.

A few of the prompts from above ("I notice …," "The artist …") work just as well with a collection as with an individual piece of art. Here, however, are some more:

The art by this artist …
This collection of paintings [drawings, sculptures] …

These paintings [drawings, sculptures] are the same because …
These paintings [drawings, sculptures] are different because …

Writing after Studying an Element of Art Composition

Another effective use of writing in our visual art classrooms is for aesthetic analysis. Whether we have been studying art elements such as line, shape, color, value, form, texture, or space, we can ask our students to write about the artwork of others or even their own art specifically looking for and commenting on that element. These prompts often lead the students to reflect on how the element affects the overall composition of the piece:

Insert the element of study where a horizontal line is given.

I see …
I notice …
When I look at my work, I see …
This work says …

The use of _____ seems to suggest …
The use of _____ makes me feel ..

Art Gallery Visits

Art galleries offer excellent programs for students which tie to our curricular objectives. During a half day, full day, or week-long program at a gallery, build writing time into your schedule. I have often sat in a gallery surrounded by works of the masters, writing. This experience is powerful for students, and museum staff are usually happy to accommodate us. Prompts to consider:

I like it here because ...   My favorite piece of artwork is ...
When I look around the room ...   The art around me makes me ...
I feel ...

In addition to the school programs offered by art galleries, many gallery websites have online tours, resources, or study guides that are available for us to use with our students. The National Gallery of Canada, for instance, has distance learning opportunities such as webinars for students and teachers to access. Many websites have extensive artist information, blogs, and virtual tours available: see, for example, the Metropolitan Museum of Art, the Van Gogh Museum, the Louvre, the National Gallery (London, England), the Detroit Institute of Art, the Rijksmuseum, and the Hermitage Museum.

Writing after Creating Art

A few years ago, I took an art therapy course at our local university. As part of this course, we created art, experimented with various mediums, and continually wrote about our experiences. Before this course, I had not thought about having students write about the creation of their art. I had used freewriting as a response to artwork already created, but not in response to their own process.

On the first day of this university class, we participated in the creation of string painting. We each had a large piece of paper in front of us and a container of black paint. Instead of a paint brush, however, we used string. The intent was not to create a particular picture or form but, instead, to explore the abstract. The spontaneity and unpredictability of this process was pleasurable: I felt relaxed and child-like. After we painted, we used crayons to add color to our creations. Our instructor then had us create a second piece and a third, all in silence, with music playing softly in the background.

The process of creating three pieces of art successively was powerful. My process changed slightly with each effort and I was surprisingly engaged and mindful. After the experience of string painting, our instructor asked us to write. What surprised me, even though I am a regular writer, was the journey of self-discovery as I reflected on the experience of string painting. I wrote about my process, my feelings as I created the art, the colors I chose, and the themes I noticed emerging in the artwork. I was genuinely shocked that my writing moved well beyond the creation of art.

This experience convinced me of the power of writing after creating art. Consider these prompts:

While I was painting [drawing,   I noticed ...
    sculpting] ...   When I look at my work I see ...

If making more than one piece of art using the same method, adopt these:
    "In the first piece ..." "In the second piece ..." "In the third piece ..."

Before this course, the art I had my students create was almost always, if not always, for a finished product. What I realized, though, is that art is so much more than the product created. It is a process: a powerful process that often leads to an expression of emotion and a way of understanding ourselves on a deeper level. Hinz (2009) states, "the healing function of the kinaesthetic component has to do with finding an inner rhythm and the release of energy" (56). This creative process can be healing in and of itself. We certainly do not always have to focus on creating a product with our students: the exploration and experience of art is powerful simply as process. Writing about the process becomes even more profound.

When we consider the complexities of our classrooms, we realize that we teach children with anxiety, children with behavior concerns, and children who have experienced loss and sometimes even trauma. Sometimes we are aware of our students' past experiences and sometimes not. Although we are not registered therapists and cannot carry out art therapy in our classrooms, we can give our students experiences through art that provide opportunities to express themselves. For some, it is a way of expending negative or excessive energy and channelling it into the creative process. Rubin (2005) suggests:

> Maybe if more children had a chance to express their feelings in and through art there would not be so many who would need specialized help for their emotional problems. Art is a very natural form of primary prevention. (329)

If you are interested in tapping into your own imagination and creative process, I recommend a Nick Bantock book, _The Trickster's Hat: A Mischievous Apprenticeship in Creativity_.

Through the creation of art, I hope to provide children with the ability to explore themselves, gain acceptance of their circumstances, and if necessary, find healing, all through genuine artistic expression. By writing after the experience, we can teach our students to be mindful during the creation of art and provide an avenue for self-discovery.

Today I felt …
My energy …
While I was creating my collage …
I chose to …
Painting [drawing, sculpting]
    makes me feel …

The colors I used …
The shapes I chose …
My lines …
I used …
This texture …

Writing after Group Art Experiences

Group art experiences can also be powerful learning opportunities for our students no matter their age. The creation of a group project forces our students to forego control, build trust, and open their minds and hearts to the creativity and expression of others. The collaboration often leads to surprising and transformative experiences. Although these experiences make wonderful team-building activities at the beginning of the year, they can be used throughout the school year to improve team dynamics and maintain an openness to others.

The premise? A group contributes to one large canvas or paper. Perhaps we gather our young students around a table covered in paper and let them run their toy cars or roll small balls through the paint. The car tires or bouncing balls create visuals on the paper as students play and create, layering and adding to what others have done.

With any age, try cooperative circle painting. The paper is laid out on the table, and various colors of paint, each with its own brush within a separate container, are available. Students begin by choosing a color and painting a circle. Silently, they move from spot to spot around the artwork, adding color and detail (lines, dots, swirls) to the artwork of their peers. The same experience can be done with doodling. The beauty of these projects where we are not trying to create a specific scene or form is that everyone, despite their artistic abilities, can participate.

I like to begin with an abstract experience. Later, though, for a different experience, you might suggest that students create something specific, perhaps a castle, a beach scene, or a forest. Often, you will see one or two people naturally take the lead. That is fine, but before you begin, be sure to set the expectation and ground rule that everyone is involved and contributes in some way.

Another variation is to use an individual piece of paper for each person instead of one large piece. After a given time with the first paper, each student passes it to the next person in the group. Eventually it returns to its original creator. (Limit each group to four or five students for best results.)

These experiences are even more interesting when completed in silence or to music. Sometimes, students are motivated or inspired by the creativity of the person beside them; sometimes, students excitedly add to something someone else has created; sometimes, students spontaneously work back and forth building on each other's efforts. Always, their work is something that couldn't have been created by one artist alone.

It is important to dialogue about this process of collaborative art before you begin. Students must go into the experience understanding that their work may be added to, changed, sometimes becoming unrecognizable from what they first created. After this discussion but before the experience, freewrite using one of these prompts:

I think I will feel …   I'm curious how …
I think it will be …   This is going to be …

After the experience, follow up with one of these freewrites either on the same day or the next:

I felt …   I liked this process because …
It felt …   I disliked this process because …
I noticed …

The freewrite could also be a reflection on the piece that was created:

I see …   The painting looks …
I notice …   I am surprised to see …

Creating or experiencing the fine arts, including music and visual art, can be powerful on its own; however, freewriting in this area heightens the creative process and may lead students on a journey of self-discovery.

11

Freewriting for Health and Wellness

"I can shake off everything as I write; my sorrows disappear, my courage is reborn."
— Anne Frank

The health and wellness curriculum is arguably of increasing importance in our complex, ever-changing world. Students are forced to face difficult realities and pressures at a younger and younger age. Technology — and social media, in particular — have added challenges that you and I didn't encounter in our formative years. I cannot imagine being a child or adolescent in today's world.

As teachers, we spend a considerable amount of time with our students. We are therefore in a wonderful position to assist them in understanding and maintaining their mental health. Where the term *mental illness* seems to carry with it a stigma (perhaps something slowly beginning to change), there is a move to promote *mental health* with a preventive approach. Teaching the content within the health and wellness curriculum can help our students learn life skills, explore their identities, and cope with stress. I want my students to become healthy, active, caring, responsible, and productive members of our community. I want them to learn healthy strategies for dealing with the stress and pressures they face.

Although health curriculums are titled differently, the general content is similar. They focus on concepts such as wellness and goal-setting; how to cope with change and stress; relationships; and identity. These topics are vital in supporting our students' overall well-being: cognitive, emotional, social, and physical.

Regardless of where you teach, the sections within this chapter will likely fit into your health curriculum. I begin with A Focus on Self (Identity, Wellness, Emotion, Mindfulness), move to A Focus on Others (Building Relationships, Managing Conflict, Considering the Effects of Technology on Relationships), and conclude with A Focus on the World (Dealing with Tragedy, Living with Gratitude, Making Connections beyond the Classroom).

In elementary school where teachers teach most subjects to their students, the health curriculum is sometimes shortchanged when time is tight. Yet the content of the health curriculum can be successfully integrated into our language arts curriculum when we ground the topics in sound literacy practices. The topics are significant and relevant to our students' lives: let's not shortchange them. In junior high or high school, there are also tremendous opportunities to utilize the themes and content of the health curriculum within our language arts or English classrooms. Powerful literature will help us do so.

Gaining Insight, Fostering Well-Being

Freewriting can become a process of self-discovery and healing. For example, when I was in junior high, I began to recognize the therapeutic value of writing as I wrote about myself and my world. Every Monday morning, I wrote to my language arts teacher in what he called our "Weekend Updates." Less than two years before, my grandmother had died, and my father had been diagnosed with multiple sclerosis. The exchanges between my teacher and me became quite therapeutic as I wrote about my grandmother's sudden death, my father's declining physical health, and the consequent changes to our household. As he did with all my classmates, my teacher wrote back to me. My adolescent-self looked forward to writing to my teacher each week and doing so helped me cope with my situation. Writing in connection to the topics within the health curriculum will assist our students in constructing meaning and learning about themselves.

Because many of the topics in the health curriculum deal with practical life skills, we may teach our older students some forms of functional writing such as business letters and job applications. As mentioned, though, the topics within the health curriculum and the skills within our language arts programs complement each other nicely. Whenever possible, connect the two to capitalize on classroom time.

What do we do with our freewrites in health?

Regardless of the grade we teach, we can build regular freewriting time into our teaching of health and wellness to enhance our students' learning. Freewriting in health class tends to be especially reflective, insightful, and profound. Since this writing is often quite personal, once again we must honor our students' choice to share all, some, or none of their writing with the class. Generally, this writing is valuable as process work and not used to create a finished product; however, if we are integrating the health topics into our language arts classes, we can ask students to choose one of their freewrites to take through the writing process.

Inspired by Literature

The use of literature is such a natural fit in this subject area. Many books deal with themes that fit into the health curriculum: emotion, self-expression, acceptance, friendship, relationships, and bullying, for example. Many of the novels on our bookshelves deal with topics of identity, loss, resilience, and courage.

I will never forget my own Grade 6 year when each girl in the class read and passed along *Are You There, God? It's Me, Margaret* by Judy Blume. It was a way to discover ourselves as girls and explore some of the changes that our bodies were going through in a safe and comfortable way. The reading of this novel provided us with the realization that we were not alone in our fears, questions, or experiences. Even more important, it sparked much discussion, helping us better understand ourselves as changing adolescents and our place in the world. Yet surprisingly to some, *Are You There, God? It's Me, Margaret* has been both banned and challenged. So have many of Blume's other books: *Blubber*, *Forever*, *Deenie*, and *Then Again, Maybe I Won't*. Her novels deal with real issues children face: friendship, bullying, religion, puberty, body image, and teenage sexuality. The books are widely acclaimed and have sold millions of copies, but most of them have been banned from some libraries. Blume also receives an alarming amount of hate mail.

And yet, by providing students with literature that reflects their realities as changing young boys and girls, we give them a means to explore their adolescence in a safe environment. When choosing a book to read, our students look to find themselves within literature through such elements as gender, cultural groups, and sexual orientation. Students tend to choose titles that reflect their own life or identity. It is also essential that we use literature to help students see beyond themselves: to connect to worlds that they would not otherwise experience, to walk in another's shoes through the pages of a book.

As students arrive from various countries throughout the world, we, as educators, must monitor our collections to ensure that they represent a range of cultures. Finding their identity within a new school, not to mention a new country with vastly different and sometimes conflicting principles and standards, is both challenging and frightening for students. Books can assist them in finding their place.

By now you are adept at creating prompts based on the literature you read. Here, however, are some effective general prompts for these books:

I am …	I am lucky …	I love …
I feel …	I dream of …	I like to be …
I wish …	I've lost …	Friendship means …
I know …	I'm nervous about …	Family means …
My life …	I fear …	My culture …

Picture Books for Use in Health and Life Skills		
Book Title	**Author(s)**	**Topic, Themes**
Aesop's Fables	Aesop	Life lessons
Alma and How She Got Her Name	Juana Martinez-Neal	Names, identity, family connections
Beautiful Hands	Kathryn Otoshi	Inspiration, creativity, dreams
The Best Part of Me	Wendy Ewald	Individuality, self-worth
The Big Umbrella	Amy June Bates, cowritten with Juniper Bates	Kindness, inclusion
The Black Book of Colors	Menena Cottin	Braille, blindness
The Blue Day Book for Kids	Bradley Trevor Greive	Encouragement, self-esteem
Don't Laugh at Me!	Steve Seskin and Allen Shamblin	Acceptance, anti-bullying
Each Kindness	Jacqueline Woodson	Friendship
Emmanuel's Dream: The True Story of Emmanuel Ofosu Yeboah	Laurie Ann Thompson	Disability, perseverance
Enemy Pie	Derek Munson	Friendship

Picture Books for Use in Health and Life Skills		
Book Title	**Author(s)**	**Topic, Themes**
Every Day Is Malala Day	Rosemary McCarney	Education, human rights, gender equality, freedom of speech
A Family Is a Family Is a Family	Sara O'Leary	Family diversity
Feathers	Phil Cummings	Homelessness, poverty
14 Cows for America	Carmen Agra Deedy	9/11, international relations, global community
From the Stars in the Sky to the Fish in the Sea	Kai Cheng Thom & Kai Yun Ching	Gender identity
Grandma's Scrapbook	Josephine Nobisso	Relationships, death
Happy Dreamer	Peter H. Reynolds	Self-worth, self-identity
The Heart and the Bottle	Oliver Jeffers	Loss
I Am Peace: A Book of Mindfulness	Susan Verde	Emotion, mindfulness
I Love My Hair!	Natasha Anastasia	Self-acceptance
In My Heart: A Book of Feelings	Jo Witek	Emotion
The Invisible Boy	Trudy Ludwig	Relationships, classroom dynamics
The Invisible String	Patrice Karst	Love, connection
Jin Woo	Eve Bunting	Family, adoption
Just the Way You Are	Max Lucado	Love, acceptance
Kid President's Guide to Being Awesome	Brad Montague & Robby Novak	Positive attitudes, identity
Malala's Magic Pencil	Malala Yousafzai	Education, human rights, gender equality, freedom of speech
The Memory Tree	Britta Teckentrup	Death, remembrance
Michael Rosen's Sad Book	Michael Rosen	Sadness, grief, loss
My Name Is Bilel	Asma Mobin-Uddin	Identity, race
My Name Is Blessing	Eric Walters	Disability, poverty
My Name Is Yoon	Helen Recorvits	Immigration, culture, acceptance
The Name Jar	Yangsook Choi	Identity, race
No One But You	Douglas Wood	Individuality, self-worth
Not My Fault	Leif Kristiansson	Bullying
One	Kathryn Otoshi	Acceptance, anti-bullying
Only One You	Linda Kranz	Individuality, appreciating life
The Other Side	Jacqueline Woodson	Friendship, race

Quiet Please, Owen McPhee	Trudy Ludwig	Relationships, the importance of listening
Sidewalk Flowers	JonArno Lawson	Gratitude, appreciating life
Small Things	Mel Tregonning	Dealing with anxiety, sadness
So Few of Me	Peter H. Reynolds	Time management
Something Beautiful	Sharon Dennis Wyeth	Gratitude
Stella Brings the Family	Miriam B. Schiffer	Family
A Stone for Sascha	Aaron Becker	Death, grief
Strong Is the New Pretty	Kate T. Parker	Girls' health, identity
A Teaspoon of Courage for Kids	Bradley Trevor Greive	Courage, encouragement
Thank You, Mr. Falker	Patricia Polacco	Gratitude
That Summer	Tony Johnston	Childhood illness, death, grief
The Thank You Book	Mo Willems	Gratitude
Those Shoes	Maribeth Boelts	Gratitude
The Velveteen Rabbit	Margery Williams	Unconditional love
You Are Special	Max Lucado	Self-worth, acceptance
What Do You Do with a Chance?	Kobi Yamada	Opportunity, courage
What Makes Us Unique? Our First Talk about Diversity	Dr. Jillian Roberts	Diversity
When We Were Alone	David Alexander Robertson	Identity, race, residential schools
Words	Lora Rozler	Friendship, bullying, choices
Zero	Kathryn Otoshi	Self-worth

A Focus on Self

This section explores the relationship between freewriting and four aspects of self — identity, wellness, emotion, and mindfulness. It recognizes how freewriting can help students explore and reflect upon their sense of self.

Identity

The topic of identity — in some form or another — seems to be in the news and media daily. Identity refers to both who we are as individuals and who we are as a collective. Our children — indeed, children in any era — search for their identities and their place in the world. Identities are affected by circumstance: birth order, family dynamics, access to resources, values, and environment. My own identity was developed in the context of being the youngest of three children and the only daughter; growing up in a family that valued books and learning; and later, experiencing my father's physical decline after a diagnosis of multiple sclerosis. If you consider your own identity, I am sure you would agree it was shaped, in part, by your circumstances: both positive and negative.

We cannot control the factors that shape our students' identities, but we can support them in their search for their authentic selves. Literature is often the springboard for discussion; writing can then follow.

I am …   I am unique because …
I like myself because …   Diversity is …

In their book *Upstanders*, Daniels and Ahmed (2015) refer to the creation of identity webs:

> These webs are visual representations of how an individual sees himself and how others see him. Identity webs can easily become a go-to strategy with your kids: they help students to understand themselves better and to activate their critical thinking and empathy. (64)

Our names go in the middle of the page and then we brainstorm details about ourselves. For example, if I was modeling my own identity web, I might talk about categories: family member (wife, stepmother, daughter, sister, aunt), roles (teacher, writer, reader, learner), ethnicity (Canadian with Ukrainian, Polish, and Czech ancestry), and then other things that apply to me, such as things I like to do (write, read, travel, visit art galleries, walk the dog, garden) or personality traits (patient, determined, compassionate). This exploration works beautifully with the freewrite prompt "I am …" either before or after the creation of the identity map. This work could also be in conjunction with literature we are reading. *Alma and How She Got Her Name* by Juana Martinez-Neal is effective because it deals with family connections, personality traits, and interests, sparking both reflection and introspection in the reader.

Helping our students to understand themselves is a powerful experience. Sara Ahmed, referring to middle school students, in particular, writes this:

> Identity is in constant question at this age. Kids are asking who they are and who they will be. They are hyperconcerned with the way others view them, and how they see themselves is continually evolving. We want them to work toward recognizing how the choices we make are grounded in our identity. (Daniels and Ahmed 2015, 84)

As we get older, part of our identity becomes tied to our roles and potential career choices. As high school students begin to make choices that influence the direction of their lives, it can be helpful for them to write about passions and interests. These freewrites can aid them in determining their purpose and goals:

I dream about …   My favorite thing to do is …
I love to …   My dream job would be …
One day I hope to …

Wellness

Wellness is another topic that dominates the health curriculum. For our very young students it includes nutrition, body image, and an active lifestyle; for our older students it also involves topics such as an understanding of substance abuse and human sexuality. Curriculum changes are being proposed in Alberta, for example, because of the current opioid crisis.

One way to promote wellness with our students is to help them to identify how good habits (or bad, for that matter) make them feel. Talking about these topics is, of course, vital. But writing, especially low-stakes writing, will give *all* students the opportunity to connect and reflect on the topics on a personal level. Here are a few appropriate prompts:

When I eat …

When I eat too much …

After exercise I feel …

After going for a walk, I feel …

After stretching I feel …

After I play _____ I feel …

Too much screen time makes me feel …

I feel tired when …

Of course, those prompts related to exercise and stretching are much more effective if the students write immediately after the activity. Get their heart rate up by taking them for a walk or run, using a *Just Dance* or *GoNoodle* video, or playing a game of floor hockey or soccer, and then have them write. Or, lead the students through some yoga or stretching before writing. The writing could potentially be on any topic, but if your goal is to have students reflect on their feelings after exercise, be sure to give them a prompt to initiate this reflection.

Emotion

It is common for health curriculums to address emotion and self-regulation strategies. By using literature and art, and by freewriting about emotion, students are better able to identify their emotions and gain insight into how they are affected by their emotions. Here are some appropriate prompts:

By its very nature, freewriting taps into the emotions of our students.

Crying makes me feel …

Laughing makes me feel …

I feel happy [excited, proud, sad, scared, angry, frustrated, disappointed, grumpy, embarrassed, worried] when …

I felt happy [excited, proud, sad, scared, angry, frustrated, disappointed, grumpy, embarrassed, worried] when …

When I am happy [excited, proud, sad, scared, angry, frustrated, disappointed, grumpy, embarrassed, worried], I like to …

When I am happy [excited, proud, sad, scared, angry, frustrated, disappointed, grumpy, embarrassed, worried], my body …

Today I feel …

It is okay to feel sad [scared, angry, frustrated, disappointed, grumpy, worried] because …

If I feel sad [scared, angry, frustrated, disappointed, grumpy, worried], I can choose to …

Mindfulness

It is essential that our students understand and accept the range of emotions they feel, including sadness, anger, and frustration, but we also want to give them the tools to deal with those emotions. The term *mindfulness* has almost become a buzzword. Regardless, mindfulness is an appropriate way to approach self-regulation with our students. We can teach them to be mindful in many situations:

before a test, when they are upset, if something worries them, and before they go to sleep. Perhaps at its simplest, *mindfulness* means being present in the moment.

Some teachers ask students to be mindful when they begin the day or return from a recess break. The students find a spot in the room to sit quietly with intention: listening and feeling their breathing, letting their thoughts come and go. Even a few minutes of mindfulness is said to be good for both the body and the brain. Teachers and students have both noticed an increase in focus, concentration, and energy after sitting mindfully for a few moments. Practising mindfulness in this setting can assist students when they find themselves in a difficult situation. When we are attentive and mindful of our situation, when we learn to become aware of our thoughts nonjudgmentally, we are more likely to be able to control our emotions, minimize stress, and deal with the situation appropriately. Breathing techniques, too, can help our students to be calm, relax, and stay in control of a situation.

Writing after engaging in a period of mindfulness is powerful. My students and I have both experienced a clarity of thought and a tendency to be more creative. Again, the writing you do could be with any of our general prompts ("I am …" or "I feel …"), but it could also be directly related to practising mindfulness:

Sitting mindfully is …   In the quiet moments …
I am mindful of …   When I focus on my breathing …
When I am mindful …

A Focus on Others

This section explores how freewriting can help students understand and deal with others: building relationships, managing conflict, and considering the effects of technology on relationships.

Building Relationships

A large portion of the health curriculum deals with relationships and all that goes along with them: interpersonal skills, friendships, and roles. Our students grapple with their identities but certainly do not live in a vacuum. As adults, most of us have grown into our identities and have become more secure of ourselves. As children and adolescents, however, our students are still exploring who they are. They are often significantly influenced by their interactions with others. To consider various relationships, they might respond to any of these prompts:

Kindness is …   When I'm with my mom [dad,
Love is …   grandma, grandpa, sister,
Friendship is …   brother], I feel …
True friends …   My family …
I knew _____ was my friend   I am an important member of my
    when …   family because …
Friends don't …   I am an important member of this
I feel [felt] included when …   class because …
I feel [felt] excluded when …   _____ is important to me
                                because …

Think of mindfulness as momentarily pressing pause.

Managing Conflict

An effective practice when teaching conflict management is presenting our students with situations and scenarios. The specific situations will vary depending on the grade level, but the idea remains the same. For younger students, the situation might be dealing with a bully on the playground; for older students, the situation might be peer pressure to drink or do drugs at a party. Students can write after role-playing or discussing the scenario:

If I was in this situation, I would …	It would be hard to …
I think I would feel …	This situation could lead to …

Considering the Effects of Technology on Relationships

For better or worse, technology has become an integral part of our lives. When you think of it, our students have not experienced a time without cellphones, computers, or tablets. As much as I appreciate the convenience and ease of technology, I also recognize its pervasiveness. In fact, there have been an increasing number of studies about its influence on our lives. Some of the concerns include a compromised attention span, anti-social behavior, difficulties forming lasting friendships, and anxiety about face-to-face communication. Discussing the potential impacts of technology can help our students understand why their parents may have rules about technology use: banning it at dinner time or limiting their screen time, for instance.

I have seen numerous programs and read many articles about families that agreed to limit or discontinue their screen time for significant periods: a digital detox, if you will. To gain a different perspective, we could facilitate a digital detox during school time or even invite students to join us for a complete digital detox (home and school) for a set time. These experiences can help us, and our students will become more aware of how the technology is affecting their daily lives — specifically, their relationships.

With or without a digital detox, students can reflect on the technology in their lives:

I like technology because …	During my digital detox, I noticed …
I don't like technology because …	
Technology can be frustrating when …	During my digital detox, it was hard to …
When I wasn't using technology, I felt …	During my digital detox, I was surprised that …

I have also heard that one side effect of social media is that we don't live in the moment. We are so busy photographing, posting, or sharing what we are doing that we find less joy in the activity itself. As well, there is an envy created by social media. When people post, they tend to post exciting events or seemingly fun moments. It may look as if our friends are having more fun than we are.

It is essential to help our students reflect on their use of social media. They can explore misconceptions, understand perceptions, and formulate their own thoughts about these matters. Helping our students consider the differences between online and personal relationships is also important. Possible prompts:

I like social media because …	When I look at my friends' posts, I feel …
I don't like social media …	

When people post things online, they …

Social media are …

Truth is …

My online friends …

My in-person friends …

This self-awareness will have an impact on our students' formation of identity and, ultimately, their interactions and relationships with others.

A Focus on the World

This section explores how freewriting can assist students in dealing with tragedy, living with gratitude, and making connections beyond the classroom. In *Powerful Understanding*, Adrienne Gear (2018) points out, "Many of our children are bubble-wrapped, not really aware that they hold a place near the top of the privilege pyramid" (143). By exposing students to experiences outside their own and by using freewriting as a tool for reflection, we can enable our students to better understand the complex world in which they live and their place within it.

Dealing with Tragedy

Every day on the news, it seems, we hear of another tragedy. Even if we choose not to watch the news, we would still be bombarded with news feeds, pictures, videos, and stories on social media. And, as much as we try to shield our students from the worst of it, from the details, we are surrounded by this news everywhere we turn. They, too, hear of things, if not from the media, then from their friends. After an event such as 9-11, the Toronto van attack, or the Humboldt Broncos bus accident, it is almost a given that our students will be made aware of what happened. The prevalence of school shootings in the United States is staggering. The Sandy Hook Elementary School shooting was especially traumatic because of the young age of the victims.

Pretending such events don't happen isn't the answer; neither is preventing our students from talking about disturbing events. Sensitive and thoughtful conversations, without a lot of detail about the event, can help reassure our students. I often think of this advice from Fred Rogers, host of *Mr. Rogers' Neighborhood*, when I am helping children deal with difficult events:

> When I was a boy and I would see scary things in the news, my mother would say to me, 'Look for the helpers. You will always find people who are helping.' To this day, especially in times of 'disaster,' I remember my mother's words, and I am always comforted by realizing that there are still so many helpers — so many caring people in this world.

You may want to read "Mister Rogers and Newtown: Quote and Image Go Viral," a *Washington Post* article by Maura Judkis (published December 17, 2012).

This perspective is one that helps our students focus on the positive in the situation, despite how tragic the circumstances might be.

Literature can also help us talk to students about events. The picture book *14 Cows for America* is a true story about a Maasai warrior who was in New York on September 11, 2001. When he returned to his village in Kenya and shared what he had experienced, the community was moved. This story, though referring to the events of 9-11, brings forth a tone of hope and comfort as a community across the world decides to help.

In addition to our delicate conversations, writing further assists our students in processing a tragic event. Sometimes when we only talk about it, students are left with more questions. By writing about it, students can explore their feelings about it more fully:

When I see [hear] the news …   The world is …
Today I feel …   The helpers …
I am confused …

Living with Gratitude

A quotation on a card sits on my desk: "Enjoy the little things for one day you may look back and discover they were the big things." When I reflect on my father, a man who was disabled for 14 years and quadriplegic for the last six years of his life, I would say this is the way he lived, how he survived: by living in the moment and being grateful for the little things.

What helps us to have gratitude? Why dedicate a whole section to gratitude in a chapter about health and wellness? We live life differently when we appreciate what we have.

Many years ago, I volunteered in Romania for a summer. I worked with children mainly at a summer camp but also in an orphanage. My biggest epiphany was how appreciative those children were of *everything*: they appreciated their interaction with adults, our smiles, the time devoted to them, the games we played, the toothbrushes, pencils, and backpacks we brought for them. I returned home and was struck by the differences in attitude of the young people in our society. Our students, who generally have so much compared to other parts of the world, sometimes take their lives for granted. I don't fault them. They are used to having what they want, when they want it. Sometimes, sharing a story, reading a book, or watching a video about something going on in another part of the world is enlightening for our students, helping them step out of their own world and into another.

As mentioned in Chapter 3, Georgia Heard's heart maps are an effective way to capture what's in our hearts. "Gratitude Heart Map" is one of her templates. Before they create their own heart maps, I have students freewrite using the prompt "I am thankful for …" This activity is especially effective around Thanksgiving, but it is appropriate at any time of the year. After the freewrite, students each create a heart map. Then, as the year goes on, students return to and add to their heart maps. The freewrite prompt "I am thankful for …" can be used effectively throughout the year. In fact, it is fascinating to see how a different time of year, a different day, or a different frame of mind can affect our writing.

Mo Willem's *The Thank You Book* is an amusing, engaging read to motivate our very young students to start thinking about gratitude. *Sidewalk Flowers* by JonArno Lawson is a touching wordless picture book which brings attention to the little things in our world. For our older students, use books such as *Something Beautiful* by Sharon Dennis Wyeth or *Four Feet, Two Sandals* by Karen Lynn Williams and Khadra Mohammed.

Making Connections beyond the Classroom

Some of the most memorable moments of my career occurred when my students and I connected with people outside our classroom. Sometimes this occurred through letter writing and sometimes through in-person visits. Regardless, these moments help our students see beyond themselves and better understand their place in the world. Aristotle once said, "Educating the mind without educating the heart is no education at all." Reaching outside ourselves and finding purpose can help educate the heart.

Students can begin by reaching out to people beyond the classroom but still within the school. I teach my students to meaningfully engage with the secretary, custodian, volunteers, other staff, indeed, everyone they encounter. We can also reach beyond our school into the community through letter writing, shared meals, and visitations.

Letter Writing: Who doesn't like receiving a letter? There are many opportunities to reach out to others in the world through writing. I have had my students write to the child we sponsored, to veterans, to a pen-pal class, and to seniors. Each of these experiences brings with it an incredible opportunity for discussion and reflection. We talk about the country and circumstances of the child we have sponsored and compare that child's world to our own. We talk about the difficult demands placed on our veterans who are away from family and would benefit from an uplifting, encouraging message. We talk about our pen pals and their school, city, or country. And we talk about the loneliness that can be experienced by some seniors and how a handwritten note might raise their spirits.

These writing opportunities are valuable in and of themselves, but the real learning occurs when students write about their experiences and reflect on the impact they have had on another person's life. Students could freewrite using these prompts:

After sending the letter I felt …	If I was alone and away from my
I wonder …	family …
I noticed …	If I had to leave my home …
I hope to …	If I got a letter …
I pray …	

They begin to experience the joy of helping others, of reaching out, and perhaps learn how fulfilling this can be.

Another group of people that may be uplifted by letters from our students would be first responders. Through research and reaching out, we can help our students learn to appreciate individuals in these difficult and demanding positions.

A Shared Meal: Food connects us to our roots: to each other. Handwritten recipes from generations past connect us through words, experience, and food. When we gather to celebrate most occasions, we share food. A shared meal is a wonderful way to help our students connect to their own roots, experience cultural diversity, and see beyond their own experience. Perhaps students could be asked to bring a dish from their own culture. Even better, each student could invite one family member to attend the meal, as well. When the room is filled with children and grandparents, parents, aunts, or uncles, the cultural connections become even stronger.

Freewriting about these experiences is powerful. Students could freewrite on the days leading up to the shared meal:

I think …	Food connects us by …
I expect …	Cooking together …
I hope …	

They could freewrite again after the experience:

I felt …	I didn't realize …
I enjoyed …	Food connects us by …
I was surprised that …	My mom's [dad's, grandma's]
I didn't know …	recipe …

When we provide our students with these opportunities to experience aspects of various cultures and perhaps encounter members of another generation (or two), they begin to form connections with their classmates and the members of their families. This experience, as well as the stories inevitably shared, help them to see others they encounter in school and out as individuals. Disagreements and tension are much less likely when we take the time to get to know one another. I have been both impressed and delighted by students' freewriting after an experience such as this. They express a range of reactions: joy, pride, gratitude, excitement, compassion. Clearly, many of them are moved by the experience. Without freewriting, though, they might not take the time to think about the event as deeply.

Visitations: Another experience incredibly valuable to our students is a visitation. Older students might visit a Kindergarten or Grade 1 class, for instance. Or, students of any age could visit a seniors' home. Students could make lunches and care packages for the homeless and then deliver them to a shelter. These intergenerational experiences are powerful learning opportunities that go far beyond our curricular objectives.

But, once again, the learning is limited if we simply visit. Writing about the visit afterwards is enlightening. My students have been brought to tears — sad and happy tears — when they read aloud their freewriting about their visitations. The joy, the sense of empathy, the compassion, and the insights that stem from these experiences are revealed and documented through the writing that occurs. Again, an understanding of individual stories is at the heart of these visits. Sample prompts:

My Kindergarten buddy …	When we gave …
The Grade 1 students …	It feels good to …
When we visited the seniors …	I wonder …
The seniors are …	I'm interested to know …

As I have sought to convey throughout this book, I believe in the power of writing. I believe, too, that its greatest potential in the lives of our students may be for the purposes of self-discovery and maintenance of an overall sense of well-being. There is no doubt about it — writing is good for our health!

As an aside, the students could also work to create a menu for the meal. Each student would be responsible for writing about a menu item with as much culinary appeal and detail as possible. They can look for menus online as examples for descriptive, delectable food writing!

12

Time to Pick Up Your Pen …

"The scariest moment is always just before you start."
— Stephen King

Freewriting found itself as one little chapter among 13 within my first book on writing, *How Do I Get Them to Write?* When I began to consider a topic for this book, I couldn't ignore the incredible responses of teachers as they introduced freewriting into their classrooms. I wanted to further explain and share the potential of freewriting to enhance our students' learning and enrich their lives. Freewriting was a transformative process in my own life: first, as a writer, and then eventually, as a teacher.

A Game-Changing Choice

When is the last time you reflected on and re-evaluated your own teaching practice? If you are now thinking of trying something new, of introducing freewriting, something else may have to go. Remember, though, our decisions about classroom practice should propel us towards our goals.

As you will recognize by my references to other resources, I use methods that work for others and add, combine, reframe, adjust, and modify them to create a program that works for me. I encourage you to do the same. We are not clones of each other; we are unique individuals with personalities and styles as varied as the fish in the ocean. Take what works for you and make it your own. Aim to adapt the ideas in this book to fit your needs and circumstances: this will ensure your most authentic teaching. We all know the saying about too much of a good thing. As much as I consider freewriting to be the game changer within my classroom, I am cautious about overusing it. Just as I would rather make freewriting time short to ensure success for all, I am cognizant of the frequency of freewriting: we must ensure we do not fatigue our students. Three times a week is manageable and effective; I recognize, however, that some weeks we might write less and sometimes more.

We have the capacity to make school a place our students dread or a place they eagerly anticipate each day. We can teach subjects, or we can teach students. We can keep our distance, or we can make connections. We can stay safe in what we have done for years, or we can take risks and try something new. We can give students what they want or what they need. If we are especially adept, we can convince them that what they need is what they want.

The Urgency of Teaching Literacy

Katherine Graham, the first female publisher of an American newspaper, once said, "To love what you do and feel that it matters — how could anything be more fun?" I am fortunate to feel this way about both literacy and teaching. I feel blessed to work with young people every day, to be inspired by them, to learn from them, to empower them, and ultimately, to make a small difference in their lives.

Brenda Augusta and Karen Cross (2017) speak of the benefits of teaching and promoting a commitment to an active lifestyle: "teaching as if our learners' very lives depended upon it — as indeed they do" (20). Could we not say the same for literacy? Reading and writing are skills that our students will carry with them throughout their lives; learning to read and write are fundamental life skills. Furthermore, humans learn through language. It's what we do. It's how we understand, process, and construct meaning. Let us teach literacy, then, *as if our learners' very lives depended upon it — as indeed they do.* Let us engage our students' minds and touch their hearts.

Why teach? "That the powerful play goes on, and you may contribute a verse."
— Walt Whitman

Bibliography

Ahmed, Sara K. 2018. *Being the Change: Lessons and Strategies to Teach Social Comprehension.* Portsmouth, NH: Heinemann.

Alberta Education. 2015. *English Language Arts K–9 Program of Studies.* Edmonton: Alberta Education.

———. 2016. "Competencies." https://education.alberta.ca/media/3272998/competency-indicators-september-30-2016.pdf.

Alessandra, Pilar. 2017. *The Coffee Break Screenwriter Breaks the Rules: A Guide for the Rebel Writer.* Studio City, CA: Michael Wiese Productions.

Augusta, Brenda, and Karen Cross. 2017. *Making Physical Education Instruction and Assessment Work: Refreshing Teaching and Learning.* Courtenay, BC: Connect2Learning.

Beers, Kylene, and Robert E. Probst. 2017. *Disrupting Thinking: Why How We Read Matters.* New York: Scholastic.

Benjamin, Amy. 2013. *Math in Plain English: Literacy Strategies for the Mathematics Classroom.* New York: Routledge.

Borba, Michelle. 2016. *Unselfie: Why Empathetic Kids Succeed in Our All-about-Me World.* New York: Touchstone.

Caine, Renate Nummela, and Geoffrey Caine. 1991. *Making Connections: Teaching and the Human Brain.* Alexandria, VA: Association for Supervision and Curriculum Development.

Campbell, Terry Anne, and Michelle E. McMartin. 2017. *Literacy Out Loud: Creating Vibrant Classrooms Where Talk Is the Springboard for All Learning.* Markham, ON: Pembroke.

Covey, Stephen R. 2004. *The 7 Habits of Highly Effective People: Powerful Lessons in Personal Change.* New York: Free Press.

Culham, Ruth. 2003. *6+1 Traits of Writing: The Complete Guide Grades 3 and Up.* New York: Scholastic.

———. 2005. *6+1 Traits of Writing: The Complete Guide for the Primary Grades.* New York: Scholastic.

Dacey, Linda. 2018. *Why Write in Math Class? K–5.* With the assistance of Kathleen O'Connell Hopping and Rebeka Eston Salemi. Portland, ME: Stenhouse.

Daniels, Harvey, and Sara K. Ahmed. 2015. *Upstanders: How to Engage Middle School Hearts and Minds with Inquiry.* Portsmouth, NH: Heinemann.

Daniels, Harvey, Marilyn Bizar, and Steven Zemelman. 2001. *Rethinking High School: Best Practice in Teaching, Learning, and Leadership.* Portsmouth, NH: Heinemann.

Dorfman, Lynne R., and Rose Cappelli. 2017. *Mentor Texts: Teaching Writing through Children's Literature, K–6.* 2nd ed. Portland, ME: Stenhouse.

Elbow, Peter. 1998. *Writing with Power: Techniques for Mastering the Writing Process.* 2nd ed. New York: Oxford University Press.

Fletcher, Ralph. 1996. *A Writer's Notebook: Unlocking the Writer within You.* New York: Harper Trophy.

Gallagher, Kelly, and Penny Kittle. 2018. *180 Days: Two Teachers and the Quest to Engage and Empower Adolescents*. Portsmouth, NH: Heinemann.

Gear, Adrienne. 2011. *Writing Power: Engaging Thinking through Writing*. Markham, ON: Pembroke.

———. 2018. *Powerful Understanding: Helping Students Explore, Question, and Transform Their Thinking about Themselves and the World around Them*. Markham, ON: Pembroke.

Goldberg, Natalie. 2005. *Writing Down the Bones: Freeing the Writer Within*. 2nd ed. Boston: Shambhala.

Grant, Maria C., Douglas Fisher, and Diane Lapp. 2015. *Reading and Writing in Science: Tools to Develop Disciplinary Leadership*. Thousand Oaks, CA: Corwin.

Graves, Donald, and Penny Kittle. 2005. *Inside Writing: How to Teach the Details of Craft*. Portsmouth, NH: Heinemann.

Heard, Georgia, 1999. *Awakening the Heart: Exploring Poetry in Elementary and Middle School*. Portsmouth, NH: Heinemann.

———. 2016. *Heart Maps: Helping Students Create and Craft Authentic Writing*. Portsmouth, NH: Heinemann.

Hinz, Lisa D. 2009. *Expressive Therapies Continuum: A Framework for Using Art in Therapy*. New York: Routledge.

Kittle, Penny. 2013. *Book Love: Developing Depth, Stamina, and Passion in Adolescent Readers*. Portsmouth, NH: Heinemann.

Lent, Releah Cossett. 2016. *This Is Disciplinary Literacy: Reading, Writing, Thinking, and Doing … Content Area by Content Area*. Thousand Oaks, CA: Corwin.

Littky, Dennis. 2004. *The Big Picture: Education Is Everyone's Business*. Alexandria, VA: Association for Supervision and Curriculum Development.

Newkirk, Thomas, and Penny Kittle, eds. 2013. *Children Want to Write: Donald Graves and the Revolution in Children's Writing*. Portsmouth, NH: Heinemann.

Ontario Ministry of Education. 2006. *The Ontario Curriculum, Grades 1 to 8: Language*. Toronto: Ontario Ministry of Education.

Pearson, P. David, and Margaret C. Gallagher. 1983. "The Instruction of Reading Comprehension." *Contemporary Educational Psychology* 8 (3): 317–44.

Rectanus, Cheryl. 2006. *So You Have to Teach Math? Sound Advice for Grades 6–8 Teachers*. Sausalito, CA: Math Solutions.

Rief, Linda. 2018. *The Quickwrite Handbook: 100 Mentor Texts to Jumpstart Your Students' Thinking and Writing*. Portsmouth, NH: Heinemann.

Ritchhart, Ron, Mark Church, and Karin Morrison. 2011. *Making Thinking Visible: How to Promote Engagement, Understanding, and Independence for All Learners*. San Francisco: Jossey-Bass.

Routman, Regie. 2014. *Read, Write, Lead: Breakthrough Strategies for Schoolwide Literacy Success*. Alexandria, VA: ASCD.

Rubin, Judith Aron. 2005. *Child Art Therapy: 25th Anniversary Edition*. Hoboken, NJ: John Wiley.

Shubitz, Stacey. 2016. *Craft Moves: Lesson Sets for Teaching Writing with Mentor Texts*. Portland, ME: Stenhouse.

Trimble, John R. 1975. *Writing with Style: Conversations on the Art of Writing*. Englewood Cliffs, NJ: Prentice-Hall.

Whitin, Phyllis, and David J. Whitin. 2000. *Math Is Language Too: Talking and Writing in the Mathematics Classroom*. Urbana, IL: National Council of Teachers of English.

Willis, Judy. 2017. "The Neuroscience of Narrative and Memory: Delivering Content — in Any Class — through a Story Has Positive Effects on Your Students' Information Retention." Edutopia. https://www.edutopia.org/article/neuroscience-narrative-and-memory.

Index